1 Man's Heart

Kenyon Healey

"3 in 1"

Book ~ Personal Assessments ~ Small Group Questions

DEDICATION

This book is dedicated to Ayva and Mia Healey.
You girls will never know how much I love you.
From the first day I laid eyes on you two, my heart
was stolen forever. I'm so honored and blessed to
say that I'm your father. I thank God every day for
two of the greatest gifts a man could ever ask for. I
pray for you daily; my love for you is
unconditional, my defense around you is
impenetrable, and my devotion to you is
inexhaustible. My prayer is that God will use you
girls mightily, and that your lives will become a
megaphone for His glory. May God's hand rest
upon you, his angels camp around you, and his love
cover you. May Goodness and Mercy follow you all
the days of your lives. Daddy loves you with all of
his heart and I'll always be your biggest cheerleader
as you fulfill God's purpose for your lives.

Daddy loves you both now and Always!

CONTENTS

KENYON HEALEY

Bookings & Social Media

Bookings:

Tiana.healey@icloud.com

Facebook:

Kenyon Healey

Grace Family Church California

Instagram:

kenyonencourage

fulfilledmarriage

couplesgear

_gracefamilychurch

ACKNOWLEDGMENTS

Tiana, Sahmya, Ayva, and Mia. The greatest treasures in my life. Thank you for your support and love.

Chapter 1

THE INVISIBLE PAGES

Let's start by defining the meaning of a diary. According to Webster's dictionary, 1828 edition, a diary is "an account of daily events or transactions; a journal; a register of daily occurrences or observations; as a diary of the weather." The Merriam-Webster dictionary defines a diary as "a record of events, transactions, or observations kept daily or at frequent intervals: journal; *especially*: a daily record of personal activities, reflections, or feelings." So, a diary can be used as a list of memories -- memories that are recorded so that someone may refer back to them in the future. I personally believe that these memories are not just recorded but sometimes they act as an invisible counselor for our future actions. Many times, we are living out - in our present state - emotions that were created five, ten or even fifteen years prior.

We must be careful not to allow an unhealthy history to dictate our present story. Diaries are a very powerful tool; if they find themselves in the right hands they can have tremendous power. But if a diary finds itself in the wrong hands, there can be tremendous pain. Be careful with whom you share your diary. Diaries are private for a reason, they are hidden for a reason, they are kept in a safe place for a reason. Everyone isn't worthy of your diary; everyone isn't worthy of the secrets of your heart. Everyone can't handle the writing on your pages: the pain, love, sacrifice, regret, passion, fear, doubt, faith, hope, insecurity, sexuality, desires.

My first piece of advice is not to give everyone access to your intimate space without making them earn it. Closeness, intimacy, information, past, history, vision, plans, ambitions, ought to be viewed as sacred. Everyone isn't worthy of that level of access in your life. Even if you don't feel valuable, your story remains priceless. Your history is unique and your responses are organic, full of life, pain and emotion, capable of transforming dead situations into motion.

Never accept the lie that a problem, issue, or struggle, was a waste of time. Every experience, tear, business deal, relationship, or endeavor adds layers of value to you. One day someone will find your diary, someone who is worthy of it, and as they peel back the layers and turn the pages, they will be overwhelmed with your power, courage, audacity, passion and love. We must find the courage to continue writing our diary, even if we haven't found someone worthy of reading our book. Just keep writing my friend!

I want to share a story with you. Imagine for a moment that you're hanging out with one of your friends and the two of you decide that you have a taste for some good old-fashioned coffee. You hop into your car and off you go to your local coffee shop. The line to purchase your most coveted drink is pouring out of the door and while standing in line your friend begins to tell you about an amazing book she just finished reading. For the next fifteen minutes she is boasting, and applauding the ideas and lessons learned from this incredible book. Finally, you receive your coffee and the two of you walk to your car and just relax for a while, talking about your lives and families. You, however, can't get that book out of your mind. The more your friend talks, the deeper you daydream about reading it. Your meeting becomes nothing more than a time for you to dream about the moment when you finally get this book in your hands, when you can turn open its pages and you can see and experience everything your friend just downloaded to you about the greatest book ever written. Your meeting finally comes to an end and you barely allow your friend to get safely out of the car before you burn rubber to your local bookstore. Then, you realize that it's no longer the 90's when you could find a bookstore within 5 minutes of your house. You quickly ask Siri where you can find the closest bookstore. And here come your directions.

You pull up to the bookstore just hoping that you'll find this book. Upon entering the store, you bypass the worker and never hear their greeting. You race up and down every aisle searching for this book; you know it has to be there, you're starting to tremble and your palms are beginning to sweat in expectation of finding that incredible book. One of the workers sees you scurrying up and down the aisles, looking rather frustrated. She approaches you and asks if there is anything she can help you find, and relieved, you answer, "Absolutely!" Once you finish the description the worker says, "I have that book. I've read it and it changed my life." She proceeds to walk over to the correct shelf; she grabs the book and hands it to you. Your eyes have become big with anticipation. Your heart is beating faster than a drummer boy. You make haste to the register to purchase the book and you frantically leave the store like a thief that is running from the law. Once in your car, you pause and take a breath -- heart pounding, hands sweating, your body temperature has risen. Here comes the moment of truth. You open the book and you are blown away. You cannot believe what you are seeing, you turn from page to page, and every page brought a new emotion, each page made you want to turn to the next. Every page made you a little more angry than before. In these few minutes, you have experienced excitement, shock, curiosity, denial, anger and betrayal.

I'm sure by now you are wondering what happened. Well, the book that she coveted so much had a beautiful cover and it was bound perfectly, but the only problem was that the book was full of empty pages. This picture is a description of many men. There are amazing men with strong bound covers, they can bring someone so much joy and happiness. They are worth purchasing; they have the propensity to make your heart flutter, and your palms sweat. But, if you're not careful you will purchase this book and fall in love with the cover, but never see the emptiness of their life's pages. They have been damaged, insecure, lonely, hurt or afraid for so many years that you will see the cover and never really explore the pages to see if there is really any content on them. Not only could there be an absence of content, but if you do happen to find content you must know what it entails. There is always a risk of opening their hearts and expecting intimacy only to leave feeling rejected because they were only able to offer you proximity.

It's very difficult for a person to lead what they need. It will be difficult for him to lead you to security if he is insecure, it will be hard for him to love you when he truly doesn't understand love. Many people have found the right thing at the wrong time and that caused it to be the wrong thing. The invisible pages of his heart are truly the diary of his soul. Traditionally speaking, women are the

7

ones that have diaries, the content would contain the secrets of their hearts, they would fill pages of books with the good, the bad and the ugly. A woman's diary in the context of intimacy, would be the keeper of more secrets than a trusted friend. Men may not write their soul wounds and successes on paper but they truly keep score in their heart. That's why men and women have to guard their hearts because our hearts will truly determine where we will end up. We must act as an umpire in regards to our hearts, making sure we don't allow balls and strikes to go unnoticed.

Now back to the story. You leave the parking lot so angry that you head immediately to your friend's house to find out why she lied to you and why she'd ever deceive you. You get to her house and bang on the door, ready to demand answers. She opens the door and to your amazement she's laughing, and her behavior brings you to the point of rage. She calms you down. "Relax, relax. I will explain everything," she says. She sits you down on the couch and begins to tell you that the objective of the book was to find out how many people are really paying attention to the fine print. At the bottom of the cover the book says, "ATTENTION: The contents of these pages are not invisible. Words will appear when you blow onto the pages." After she explains this, you are left in utter shock. "So, you're telling me that I can't see the words because I haven't, literally, blown on the pages?" Yes, she replies. You believe you are being punked at this point, but your friend appeals to your curiosity: "No, just try it." As you begin to blow air/life onto the pages, to your amazement, the words on the pages are revealed. And as long as you are blowing words continue to appear.

This is a picture of a man's heart. A man is not willing to allow just anyone to easily find him, or grant her unlimited access into his life. Having permission to read the secrets of his heart is considered a privilege, not a right. What man would be so foolish to permit just anyone to be in his secret place, potentially leaving himself exposed and vulnerable? In order to truly see a man's heart, you must know how to blow life into him.

The fine print for a man is sometimes giving someone a small secret of his heart to see how the recipient will handle it. The recipient's response will typically dictate if he will open that vault up ever again. Men will open up, but that window isn't open very long. It's like blowing on the pages; you have to read correctly what's written while blowing, once you stop blowing the window closes. Meaning, you can't just speak life into him once and expect unlimited access to his heart. You must perpetually speak life/blow on his pages in order for him to remain consistent in trusting you with his most intimate self. Men will allow full access to their hearts when the person holding the book has safe and trustworthy hands. Even if a woman possesses safe hands, it doesn't guarantee that the process of disclosure speeds up. Nor does it promise that a man will freely disclose his heart. It's a slow but steady process. View intimacy with a man as a marathon, verses, a sprint.

Most men have lived with invisible pages for so long that they themselves believe the pages are blank and hold no true content. It's not until someone comes along and blows on their life, whether it's a family member, girlfriend, spouse, friend, co-worker, counselor or clergy member. The people who blow truly life-changing air are the ones who make the decision not to keep score. They refuse to judge him. They don't keep a log of all his poor choices, and they don't find pleasure in telling him how unworthy he is. It's at this point a man realizes there's more in himself than he realized. That his past doesn't have to predict his future.

We all have a hidden diary in our hearts and these pages are full of content that exposes who we really are. The saying is true, there is more to you than what meets the eye. Hidden pages don't necessarily mean someone is lying, sometimes it's due to fear, ignorance, insecurity, pain, rejection, molestation, early exposure to pornography, verbal abuse, physical abuse, emotional abuse, psychological abuse, loneliness, negative self-image, drug use, same sex attraction. Any of these things and many others can cause us to hide and not expose our true nature because we are afraid of being rejected. Many of us have lived as amateur actors on a professional stage. We know how to walk the walk and talk the talk. We play the role, many times because we feel that if someone really knew everything about us they wouldn't love us, or that they would reject or judge us. We believe this because in most cases it's true. People are quick to judge others, but not quick to evaluate themselves. If people spend more time evaluating themselves, it will leave them less time to judge others. I'm pretty sure we all have enough issues in our own lives that would leave very little time to worry about someone else. We judge others while we hide behind our own masks in order to feel safe, and keep life as "normal" as possible. But as a result, we become nothing more than the living dead, the invisible pages of the book with no life-giving air.

When a person is the living dead, they can survive and cope for a long time. But eventually they will run out of strength, and their house of emotions will crumble and become nothing more than a pile of rubble. Even though they are a pile of brokenness, they are still valuable. For example, Michelangelo once said that when he sees a block of wood or material he doesn't see the dirty, disformed object. He said, he begins to cut away the obscure, the damaged, the molded, the sharp, and he will cut over and over again until he sets free the beautiful bird stuck in the midst of an old block of wood. Many will miss the beautiful bird because of the stump. We must be able to see the "stump diaries" of a man and not discard him because he may be rough, dirty, broken or hurt. We must be willing to cut things off and clean things up until a person is free to live a beautiful life. Michelangelo put it this way, "Every block of stone has a statue inside it and it is the task of the sculptor to discover it."

Lastly, as we conclude this analogy we must ask, why were these people so excited when they read the invisible pages of their book? What made them want to tell the world that this book was incredible? Well, I believe that the book that has invisible pages is a person that desires freedom so bad they are willing to die for it, they want truth so bad they're willing to crawl over broken glass, walk through fire, leap from a building, cut their arms, put a gun to their head or take a life. These people have reached the brink of destruction and for the first time in their lives they see a light at the end of the tunnel that isn't an oncoming train. It's the path to physical, psychological and emotional freedom. Not freedom through natural death but freedom of the soul.

It's comparable to the man living on death row without the possibility of parole and on the night of his scheduled death, he receives a stay of execution from the governor. His heart is completely shocked and he believes for a moment that there may be a second chance, the possibility of a new life, new air, a new sun, a new wind, and a new beginning. This experience is what these men felt when they truly looked at their hearts, seeing the good the bad and indifferent. They saw opportunity; they saw the possibility of redemption. To restore the lost boy, the hurting child, the lonely man, the rejected father, the down cast brother, or the fallen soldier. Oh, but now they realize, even though they have been hurt, broken, ridiculed, and rejected, they still have value and they are deserving of true love, and this love can change their lives forever.

Chapter 1

Personal Assessment & Small group questions

Personal Assessment

1. What is your heart full of? Love, Fear, Joy, Hate, Sorrow, Happiness? Why are you full of that particular emotion? *(Give details don't hold back!)*

_____

_____

_____

_____

_____

DIARY OF A MAN'S HEART

2. What unhealthy patterns have you seen displayed in your life as a result of your diary's content? In other words, how have the hidden elements in your life affected your relationships?

_____

_____

3. Now that you know that there is a diary in your heart full of content, what are you going to do about it? *(This step requires you to obtain an accountability partner to hold you accountable to your commitment!)*

_____

_____

_____

_____

_____

_____

_____

_____

Small Group Questions

1. Why are we all here?

2. What are your personal goals from this *Diary of a Man's Heart* small group?

3. Do you see a need for positive change in your life? If so, in what areas?

4. Who infuses life into you on a daily basis?

5. What's the most pressing issue in your heart? *(You can't be embarrassed if you want true change!)*

6. Do you believe you are worthy of love and able to give it properly?

Group Activity

Materials needed: Pieces of paper that are all the same size and color, pencil or pens. Provide something to place all the pieces of paper inside of.

Everyone writes down a secret they don't want anyone to know. Fold them up and place them in container provided. Afterwards, the facilitator will read all of the ANONYMOUS pieces of paper one by one and the group will discuss how to overcome them!!!

Chapter 2

THE SILENT CRIES

Can you imagine walking down the street and seeing every man you walk pass crying at the top of his lungs? I don't know about you, but I'd first think some major crisis has taken place because this isn't the norm anywhere you go. Or, what would you think if you were to walk into a gym and there were a group of men playing basketball and when the ~~~~ ends, the losing team cried as

the NBA championship? And yet,

kup game at the local gym. What if

24

a guy asked a girl on a date and when she politely declined he began to cry and weep? I don't know about you but I would be taken aback by this. Granted, many of these examples are hyperbole but they illustrate a key principle.

Our society as a whole doesn't expect to see men cry. We expect men to be strong, courageous, hard workers, fixers, and spider killers. Men are expected to be the ones that run to the battle, not from it. Men are supposed to be the defenders of the kingdom. But what happens when the champion loses? What happens when the soldier is injured? What happens when the King feels as though he has lost his crown? I want to submit to you that if the man loses his position of power he may begin to feel as though he's lost his identity. It's very difficult to separate the soldier from the battlefield, or the champion from the ring, or the King from his castle.

Have you ever noticed how some of the greatest athletes have struggled to retire? Here's a list of some EXTRAORDINARY athletes that came out of retirement: Michael Jordan (NBA) came out of retirement, twice. George Foreman (boxing), Brett Favre (NFL), Floyd Mayweather (Boxing), Roger Clemens (Baseball), Mark Martin (NASCAR), Pele (Soccer), Magic Johnson (NBA). Many of the most successful men in the sports world find it very difficult to separate their gift from their person. Their gift becomes their actual identity in many cases. Men are designed to take ownership, they are designed to build, shape, mold and conquer. The idea of retiring can be quite emotional for a man. Take away his vocation, and he feels lost in many cases, as though he's lost his sense of self. His life may go from a full sprint to a fatigued trot. This scenario also applies to a man's heart. He hides his true self there, injure a man in his heart and soul, he will transition from conversation, to frustration, to anger and then he will become mute. He will try to restore it because it means so much to him, but after a while, he will stop trying, he will "officially" retire when it comes to you.

One of the greatest ways to hurt a man isn't by physically beating him up but by silencing his voice. To cause a pain so deep that he no longer speaks life, he no longer desires to create, he no longer desires to fight, he begins to have a silent cry, a nonviolent protest. Not with picket signs and marches but with SILENCE. Men have the ability to change the world by the words they speak. And this world has changed one family at a time. It starts with young boys without a father, or maybe a dad who lives in the house with him but he's the farthest thing from being a father. Or, a young boy being molested, verbally abused, neglected, teased or rejected. He will either join society and find his way by grace or he'll become a part of a perpetually broken justice system. That young man is likely to wander into manhood without a voice and without a sense of purpose. It's not his fault, it's just the reality of many people's lives.

The young man becomes a father and now has to raise a child when he himself never experienced a father. What does he say to his child?

How does he learn how to hold her? How to give her affection? How to cuddle her when she cries? How to show empathy when she's scared of her own shadow? How to listen when she just wants to talk about ponies and the little boy at school who "looked" at her? How to allow her to play dress up and do makeovers on him without feeling insecure as a man? This man, who was once just a boy, was silenced long ago by the absence of a voice in his life. He has grown up affected by the silent cries of his father as well. So in reality it's not only the silence of the man that affects the relationship, but also the lessons his father was unable to teach or pass down to him growing up.

The inability of his own father's silent cries represents the lack of ears for a man to speak into. When a man needs to share his heart, where does he go? Who does he talk to? Will he have to fight through shame and embarrassment just to share a thought? Men usually don't find it easy to share their secrets, they are sometimes not only ashamed but they are not trusting. Many people have tried to share and they were not met with an understanding ear but a judgmental voice and calloused heart. Silent cries say that there is no one to share their most intimate thoughts with. Someone they trust so much that image means nothing. Many men die with hundreds of unspoken conversations in their hearts, not because they don't want to tell anyone, but as a result of not knowing someone trustworthy enough to love them despite them being fallible. Many men lean upon their faith in order to overcome this seemingly insurmountable obstacle, while others believe that time will heal all wounds. A wise man once told me that time doesn't heal all wounds, it heals some, cements some and leaves a scar on others. Taking away the voice of the man, not only affects the man, but everyone that he is supposed to speak life into while he's alive.

If your life was a wall and bricks represent the hurts and pains in your life, every problem, struggle and issue would be a brick. Over time that wall can reach really high; time may become the cement that rests between the blocks to hold up all the hurt and pain in your life. So, many men walk around carrying 100-foot walls to their jobs, to the ball game, to relative's houses, and into relationships. Sometimes you can date a guy and he can seem so mean or distant. The problem is that some of these men are great people but their walls prevent them from showing you their true selves. So, in theory you never met them, you met the hurt and pain of their past. You've met the silent cry, not the confident voice. That voice was silenced at some point. You met the wall, judged the wall, and told the wall it's too hard, immovable, unchanging, while never asking, how did that wall get there? This is the tragedy of the diary. The hidden pages can prevent someone from living out who they truly want to be and it can cause the world to never experience the uniqueness of that individual. In essence you rob the world of YOU!

Just because a wall exists, doesn't mean it can't be torn down! It takes more time to build a wall than it does to tear one completely down, if you have the right equipment. Many men want their walls torn down but don't have the proper tools to do so. Tearing down walls is messy, time consuming, and hard work. But it can be done. Most men are taught to be a hammer. I heard it once said that if the only tool you have is a hammer, everything will look like a nail. Men must be taught to add tools to their toolbox of life. These new-found tools will assist men emotionally and psychologically as they heal and grow. Women are in a unique position to help men discover these new tools in a safe and nurturing environment.

I don't know about you but I want to know what's behind the wall, I want to know if I can become great! I want to see how things will change if I step from behind the curtain, no longer lie about who I truly am, and no longer give power to the opinions of those that truly don't love me. I'm begging you to come from out of the darkness, come into the light where all can see that you are under construction and incomplete. Nevertheless, on your way of becoming something great, memorable, and awe-inspiring, DARE TO BE

YOU!

Chapter 2

Personal Assessment & Small Group Questions

Personal Assessment

1. What in your life has silenced your greatness?

_____

_____

_____

_____

_____

_____

2. When you assess the wall in your heart,
   what are the individual bricks made of?
   (Each brick represents an experience)

3. Who are you? Who do you want to be?

DIARY OF A MAN'S HEART

_____

_____

_____

_____

_____

_____

Small Group Questions

1. What will it require for you to come out of the shadows?

2. What will it require for you to feel safe to ask questions, and communicate your true feelings?

3. How do you handle failure?

4. Do you have trusted family/friends that are trusting ears? *(These are the people that can hear, hold, and advise your secrets)*

Chapter 3

BEHIND THE MASK

There was a very funny movie that was made in 1994 entitled, "The Mask." Ian Pugh wrote a plot summary for this movie and he says, "Stanley Ipkiss is a bank clerk that is an incredibly nice man. Unfortunately, he is too nice for his own good and is a pushover when it comes to confrontations. After one of the worst days of his life, he finds a mask that depicts Loki, the Norse night god of mischief. Now, when he puts it on, he becomes his inner self: a cartoony romantic wild man. However, a small-time crime boss, Dorian Tyrel, comes across this character dubbed "The Mask" by the media. After Ipkiss's alter ego indirectly kills his friend in crime, Tyrel now wants this green-faced goon destroyed."

Many people live their lives as "the mask" instead of their true selves. Sometimes in life we will feel insecure, embarrassed, ashamed, unconfident about who we really are. In a world that glorifies perfection, we endeavor to become what the "world" wants versus being the best version of ourselves that we are capable of being. We join the race to perfection when no one can reach the unattainable goal. We strive for the unachievable and punish and beat ourselves up when we fail at a goal that we knew from the onset was unreachable. The real question we must ask ourselves is, why? Why set a goal that we know is unrealistic? Why try to obtain a body type that mimics the supermodel on television, but isn't natural to your God given shape? Why try to look like the magazine? Or, attempting to look like the woman on the runway? Why pretend that the pictures aren't photo shopped?

Are you not enough? Are you not beautiful and valuable just the way you are? Why pretend that celebrities don't have issues? Why change your goofy personality to cause someone to like you? Why not just be yourself? Why not say, forget what the world thinks, I'm going to be who I am, and if you don't like who I am or what I look like, who cares? This concept seems like a no brainer. But we all know it's the farthest thing from the truth. I know countless men that wear masks because it allows them to become someone else for a moment, it allows them to fit in, the mask gives them a moment of acceptance. The problem is that fads, crazes and trends change and people can be as fickle as the wind. So what is popular today will be unpopular next month. So, the moral of the story is that you can wear a mask today to appease people we do or do not know, but you run the risk of being out of style next season. We unconsciously begin to reinvent ourselves every new season. I believe we embrace life and personality makeovers like the seasons and try to pursue the elusive perfection because we think it will bring us a moment of happiness or acceptance.

What if someone told you that in order to be happy you will have to lose everything you have? What if happiness would come only at the brink of the devastation of your mind, will or emotions? What if the pursuit of personal glory was all a lie? What if self-denial, abandonment, and surrender were the true remedy for this life? What if you knew that perfection wasn't an option on this side of eternity but fulfillment was? What if you knew that you had what it takes to be genuinely fulfilled? When you honestly assess yourself, you recognize you don't have much hope left in you, your tank is almost empty and you're running your life on fumes. You are trying to persevere, trying to salvage as much of your life as possible. Shouldn't you save yourself at all cost? And pursue happiness while abandoning all that stands in your way. But innately you know everything you've been taught up to this point is beginning to collide with the reality of life. Can I truly achieve fulfillment in life by pleasuring myself and never denying myself? NO! Can I have true fulfillment while wearing a mask? NO! Fulfillment is mixed with the ability to say no to yourself. Fulfillment is intimately connected to your ability to deny what makes you happy for what is healthy and right. Fulfillment for a man is achievable but it will take everything you have to acquire it? Do you still want it? Would you still fight for it? If you knew that the mask's fakeness and pretentiousness could come off and you'd be safe, if you told someone that you were a liar, a thief, a drunk, drug addict, verbally abusive, physically abusive, neglectful, addicted to pornography, mean spirited, promiscuous, disabled, un-intelligent, unable to read and write, insecure, lonely, homosexual, diagnosed with a disease or STD, a bad mother, an absent father, a broken husband, a neglected wife. What if you were safe? Safe to tell the truth, knowing in your heart that telling that truth wouldn't make all your problems go away immediately, but that revealed truth would begin a journey toward true fulfillment and healing?

Would you fight? Would you have the courage, the unmitigated gall to say enough is enough, I love myself too much to wear this mask anymore. I'm not going to stay down; I may be on my back but on my back, I am now positioned to look up. I might be on my knees but I'm in a position to pray for a better tomorrow. Can you fight for that? Can you get back in the ring one more time, for **YOU!** No one else, for **YOU!** I believe that one day we have to face the mask. Life may knock us down and beat us up, but we cannot lose hope. Martin Luther King Jr. once said, "If you can't fly, then run, if you can't run, then walk, if you can't walk, then crawl, but whatever you do, you have to keep moving forward." Moral of the story, we cannot quit! I implore you to fight for your life, fight for your identity, fight for your family, fight for your marriage, fight for your salvation, fight for true fulfillment, fight for your tomorrow.

If we kill the enemy within, we have no need to fear the enemy unknown. This mask can be removed and we can be honest and vulnerable again. It's time to wake up, there's a big world out there and it's calling your name, but only you can hear its voice. I want you to awaken to the notion that being free isn't an allusion or pipe dream! It's a decision that failure isn't final, and setbacks are the springboard to your come back. That failing forward is an option. So, what if I don't have it all together? I'm not the smartest, best looking, most talented, charismatic, charming, skillful, articulate, well studied, educated, wealthy, or popular. But, what I do have is a dream, passion, vision, hope, love, sincerity, work ethic, drive, and a belief that I was created for more than what I am today. My book is still being written! Don't close the book of my life just because you don't like the chapter or page you picked me up on. Take the time to read the whole book, the good, bad, and ugly.

If you can't handle the content of my pages, you are not worthy of carrying me. Don't try to buy my book if you're not willing to read all the pages, don't pick me up as a traveling read, or collect dust on a shelf. I need someone that wants a book that has an introduction, beginning, middle, and end. It's a full read, no shortcuts. All pages are divinely inspired and they require a partner, friend, and confidant, not a lazy reader! You must say of yourself, if you stick with me to the end I assure you, at the end WE WIN! And they must believe that you are a worthy read and the mask was only a false camouflage. This has to be your testimony, "I fight for a greater cause, and my fight isn't my own." I trust that I've been designed for a purpose and I need people around me that can see the blue jay inside of the old dirty stump of wood. Someone that can believe in me when life hits me hard and I don't believe in myself! I'm taking off the mask, I'm worthy of exposure, **YOU** are worthy of living out loud.

Join me as we come out of the closet, out of the closet of low self-esteem, insecurity, oppression, depression, anger, jealousy, addiction, control, fear, doubt, unbelief, pain, trepidation, inconsistency, and judgment! Are you ready? On your mark, get set, GO!!! Take off that MASK!!! LIVE FREE!!!

Chapter 3

Personal Assessment & Small Group Questions

Personal Assessment

1. Do you feel like you are wearing a mask in life? Why?

_____

_____

_____

_____

_____

DIARY OF A MAN'S HEART

2. Is there anything in your life that is preventing you from becoming the best version of yourself? How can you make adjustments to free yourself? *(List them and elaborate)*

DIARY OF A MAN'S HEART

3. When your mask comes off, describe the type of person you see in the mirror?

DIARY OF A MAN'S HEART

Small Group Questions

1. When you realize that someone is wearing a mask, what do you do? Why do you react or respond that way?

2. If the person wearing a mask is ever exposed, how do you respond?

3. Do you find that you can judge people easily, but yet you don't critique yourself with that same level of justice? If you answered yes, give an example and explain why you hold yourself to a different standard.

4. If you've ever worn a "ma
   mask did you choose and why

5. Why do you think people compare
   themselves to other people? Why do couples
   compare themselves to other couples? Why
   is this a dangerous habit?

Chapter 4

DO YOU RESPECT YOUR LIFE'S SEASONS?

Many times in our lives we will make decisions based upon inaccurate premises. One of those beliefs is that being unmarried is a stain, a badge of dishonor, that it is troublesome, un-natural, foolish, crazy or even taboo. To some people, being single may not be easy, but it is one of the most important seasons of one's life. In most cases, women are the ones who consistently discuss their relationship status - it's a constant topic of conversation. But what fascinates me is that those women are (most likely) going to marry a man. So shouldn't this conversation be just as important in the men's circles? Why isn't it? The diary is that women have hundreds of conversations about being single, and men just live their lives until they're married. Most men never even question why they're single. They just go on with life because singleness to them isn't an issue, it's just a part of life. The problem is that something that we don't think about, we typically undervalue.

So, many people are married to ideas, dreams, rules, expectations, opinions and notoriety and yet they're not married to reality. Millions of people every day marry, date, get engaged and even stay married to an idea and never tell themselves the truth. I'm not sure what's worse: to leave a relationship or pretend while you're in one. Both scenarios are a reflection of disconnectedness.

So let's first talk about the myth of singleness. As I said before, singleness is one of the most important seasons of one's life. People who are unhappily married will try to force you to get married. They will analyze why you are single rather than focus on their own issues. I read once that people and relationships are like flies. The fly on the outside of the screen door wants to get on the inside of the house, and the fly on the inside wants to get on the outside of the house. I've also noticed single people who desperately want to be married and married people who desperately want to be single. I want to encourage a paradigm shift. This shift didn't occur in my own life until after my personal life and relationship fell apart. I truly believe that tragedy, pain, hurt, and disappointment, all work together for our benefit. Every single and every married person should spend so much time tending to their life, they don't have time to notice the relational status of someone else's. I'm not even talking about cheating, abuse, addictions, or abandonment.

Let's unpack this perspective. I'm sure many of you ladies are thinking, "Yeah, tell him...Tell him how to tend to his garden," and your interpretation is that the garden is you. But no, I'm actually talking about "his garden," meaning "his OWN life." Even though I'm asking him to evaluate himself, if you are in a relationship, you should read this together. Now, why should a man focus on himself and NO ONE ELSE? Because he CANNOT LEAD what he NEEDS! He's incapable of leading well, when he needs the exact same thing he's expected to give. For example, if I don't have any money to buy gas for my own car, how can I give you money to put gas in your car? How can I give you what I can't provide for myself? In order to give it, I must first have it. But I can not only have what I need; I must have overflow so that when I give some away, I'm not left with a need of my own. Many times, we put expectations on people to lead. Unfortunately, the person, in an effort to please someone else, will steal what they do not have in order to fulfill the other person's need. When a man is empty, but feels the emotional, mental and physical weight placed on him to give to you, he will steal the tiny bit of energy he has left to meet your need instead of simply telling you that he doesn't have what you need. The result is that you are fulfilled and he is left empty and exhausted. I don't even think women know they are taking what their men don't even have. I just think it never crosses their mind to ask. Why would you ask for something that you know I don't have? Maybe they don't have any clue that their man is living on an empty tank, maybe they are so selfish that his condition, fulfillment and happiness is the least of their concerns. Whether the motivation is pure or vindictive, the man may begin to resent her. Sometimes a man just needs a break, a moments rest. If he isn't granted this short pause he will conclude that you can never be satisfied.

Let's take this one step further: not only will you never be satisfied; he will never feel like enough. If I give and give and give, but I am never replenished, I will no longer desire to give. Because deep down, we all believe that if we give we should receive. Sometimes you give and you're expecting something in return, but what you receive may not be what you expected. This will cause me to resent the recipient because in my view, I never received anything of value in return. What should a man do when he has given everything and you are still empty or half full? At what point can he tell you, "I've given everything. Maybe the issue isn't what or how I'm pouring, but the container that I'm pouring myself into?" How can he tell you that you have so many holes in yourself, that whenever he thinks he's filled you, he can just look down on the ground and follow the trail of his efforts spilled on the floor? This is why, being healed of issues and injuries are important. Our past many times can leave "holes" in our emotions that can cause issues in the future. Men and women are walking around as though they are fine China - valuable, with no defects and no cracks, and yet neither have had the courage to come out of the China cabinet to be used and appreciated. We know in our hearts that we are not fine China, we know in our hearts that we are paper plates and plastic cups. We look deep within ourselves and we see the issues, problems, fears, and waywardness. Our conclusion is that we don't have true value, so we overcompensate by trying to give and give and give, but what we are giving is nothing more than a mirage. It looks good, but has no intrinsic value. Instead of really "becoming," we spend our time blaming everyone else for why we are the way we are. It always fascinates me that people can find so many words when speaking negatively about someone but can never seem to find any words to share their own sinful ways. That puzzles me. Even relationally. We as men are far from perfect, and in that same breath, so are women. If everyone will spend more time acknowledging their own issues, and ACTIVELY changing themselves, they will find that they have very little time left to talk about someone else. We all must respect our season. The toughest season is typically the one where we must evaluate our internal character. That's why our season of singleness is so important.

Are we (men) truly respecting our season? I

think one of the biggest culprits against the health
and wellbeing of men is the inability and or fear of
being alone. Many men struggle with being alone.
We will fill up our time, energy and emotions with
other things in order to avoid confronting our
loneliness. Sometimes, it's because being alone
forces us to face ourselves; and for many, that is a
daunting task. In order to respect this season, you
must understand the purpose of it. For a man, being
single, is the opportune time to build his internal
and external life. His internal attributes would be
his character: wisdom, patience, love, forgiveness,
consistency. His external attributes include getting
an education, having a job, managing money and
time, securing housing of some type, volunteering,
etc. Respecting your season will allow you to
develop as a man. This is the season in which you
build a foundation that a family will be able to stand
upon with confidence and security. Ladies, if I can
give you one small piece of advice on this point. I
submit to you: a man would rather be alone than to
be with someone that makes a living out of tearing

him down. Using him to the last drop, only to remind him that he was never able to fill you up.

Lastly, let me submit this final thought about seasons. A man needs every SEASON and every LESSON; a woman cannot grow a man up. Men must be forced to live with their decisions. They must be forced to sit with themselves long enough to recognize and accept the truth that they discover about themselves. Many times, women are so accustomed to picking up the pieces and "rescuing" people, that they can actually hinder a man's development and the training that life is providing. Men, we have egos and pride, and sometimes those shrines need to come crashing down and we need to be alone with the rubble. Why? Because being alone without distractions or someone to hold us up emotionally will cause us to look at how we process life and ask ourselves, if we are ready to acknowledge who we are and what we have become and take massive action to change our lives, families and careers?

The fullness of time is a man's best friend. If you undercook chicken there will be several consequences: First, it will be nasty. second, the consistency will be uneven; and lastly, it will make you sick. That's how it feels to be with an "undercooked" or "underdeveloped" man. It will be a nasty, uneven, and unhealthy relationship. Don't blame the man because you refused to check and see if he cooked long enough. You will only be satisfied when you've connected yourself to someone that has maximized his singleness, and built himself internally and externally.

Sometimes we are so hungry in life, we will just eat anything and call it food. We will date and have sex with anyone and call it a relationship. Just because he walks, talks, and can have sex, doesn't mean he's a man. No more than a dog walking on its hind legs makes it a human. I hope you understand what I'm saying - there is a time for everything in its proper season. Seasons come and go, but every season is important. We must have the maturity to allow seasons to accomplish what they came for. The fullness of time is the time required to produce optimal results, no matter how long it takes. This is called valuing the process, and as a result, we'll one day be pleased with the outcome.

Chapter 4

Personal Assessment & Small Group Questions

Personal Assessment

1. What season are you in right now? Explain what that season looks and feels like.

_____

_____

_____

_____

_____

2. What have you learned from your "best" and "worst" seasons of life?

3. Have you given so much away in life that you've found yourself wanting? When did you allow that to happen? How can you make immediate changes that will make your life healthier?

_____

_____

_____

_____

_____

_____

_____

_____

_____

DIARY OF A MAN'S HEART

Small Group Questions

1. What season of life are you currently in?

2. How did you come to that conclusion?

3. Are you fulfilled in this season? Why or why not?

4. Have you respected your life's seasons? Why or why not?

5. If we know that life is a series of seasons, what causes us to be impatient in some of those seasons?

6. How can we maximize every season in life going forward?

Chapter 5

SHOULD I STILL BE INSECURE?

Ladies, the premise of this chapter is the fact that a man having you doesn't necessarily mean that he feels confident that he has you wholly, completely and in every way. I want to tell you a story about my experience at the gym.

One day I was working out as I always do. This particular day was back attack. That just means it was back day, so that was the focus of all my exercises. Anyway, while I was doing deadlifts I noticed a couple working out right next to me; they were doing back exercises as well. I was going heavy that week so I had 405 pounds on the bar for my deadlift, and I weighed about 193 pounds at the time. I wasn't a small guy but I wasn't massive either. Well, I noticed that the husband (or boyfriend) was lifting a weight that was much lower than my weight, and the woman had noticed the amount of weight on my bar so she was watching to see if I could lift it. As I began lifting I could see her watching. She wasn't staring as though she was checking me out - it genuinely looked like she was shocked that I didn't kill myself lifting that much weight. Needless to say, her man took notice, immediately ended their workout and they left the gym. Now, I don't know the nature of their relationship or their previous experiences with one another. I'm not sure if she had a pattern of watching guys or if this was something he had never experienced with her. I don't know if there was cheating or flirting in the past or not. I don't know a lot about them, but I do know he made her pick up her stuff and walk out of the gym.

My question is: should he be insecure? I know people's initial response is that if your woman is with you and loves you don't worry about it. But, is it that easy? If his girl is looking at another man work out and he knows that that guy's body looks better than his, is he justified to feel insecure? Do you think your man would be insecure in a similar situation? I believe many men are insecure in their relationships because they are not reassured that their women's eyes are only for them. Women will see a guy on TV or a movie and become excited talking about how good he looks. But her man hasn't heard such words uttered about him. They get a simple "baby you know you're cute. You know I love you." I'm sorry, but that isn't good enough! I want "GOD you look good!" or "JESUS, you bad!" You see what I'm saying? Why does the stranger on TV get this reaction when your man is the one that has to live with you and deal with you? I'm just saying. Should he still be insecure? Do the women play a role? I'm not saying you should take full responsibility for his insecurity, but make it a point to ensure your man knows he's the only one, that he is everything you desire.

Could the day come when both people in a relationship are so committed to one another and want to make sure the other person feels secure in every way? When both people ask each other daily, "What can I do to let you know I only have eyes for you and I'm yours exclusively?" Men don't like to say they feel insecure but our actions will tell you if we are. If we say that we feel like you're looking at other people, going out of your way to draw attention, or dressing too revealingly, don't just shut us down as though we're tripping. Ask him why he feels that way and why he's insecure with you, and really listen to his answer. Avoid getting defensive and you might find that he has observed enough to justify some of his conclusions. I'm not saying all of his conclusions are accurate because we don't always judge accurately. But, many times what we feel is a direct result of our perceived reality. I watch men stare down women every day at the gym. It's like open season for hunting with an unlimited supply. Women bend over knowing guys are right by them and their men are sitting there seeing other guys check out their women. Why would you want your man to experience that? Women, you know what makes certain parts of your body look a certain way, so when you play that up, it appears as though you're looking for attention. Many tell me, "I just want to look good for my man." Has it ever crossed your mind that your man can't really enjoy what you have on because he's watching every other man enjoy it as well? I'm not saying you can't be sexy. I just believe we have to bring back a certain level of modesty! Let your man know that you are his and you want to make his eyes jump. That he has no reason to be insecure because you are only his! Small changes can lead to big results.

Chapter 5

Personal Assessment & Small group questions

Personal Assessment

1. Can you locate any areas in your life where you're insecure?

_____

_____

_____

_____

_____

2. Do you look around at other people or relationships and secretly compare? Why or why not? How do you feel making these comparisons have helped or harmed you?

3. Do you try to highlight certain areas of your
   life because you think they will cause others
   to find you more desirable or attractive?

Small Group Questions

1. Where does insecurity come from?

2. How do you typically handle your insecurities?

3. Have insecurities caused any adverse effects in your life?

4. How have we tried to draw attention to ourselves?

5. Have you lost confidence in your relationship?

6. Has something happened in your past that causes you to be insecure or have a lack of trust? How can you recover and heal from these injuries?

Chapter 6

LIFE SENTENCE

This chapter of the diary deals with the physical, psychological, and spiritual ability of men to begin a new normal.

Men all over the world are locked away, hidden in what we call "prisons." Many who are locked away deserve to be. But there are prisoners serving a great deal of time for very small, non-violent offenses. The worst case and we all know that they exist, are those that are locked away and they never committed a crime to begin with - those who have been falsely accused or set up by a system rigged against them. Our government has prisons in place to ensure the "safety" of society. If someone breaks a law and they are caught, the idea is that a person must pay for their crime, whether it be with jail time, fines, community service, or other programs.

This chapter doesn't deal with the innocent, but the guilty. As a man, what happens when you are guilty of wrongdoing? You may have made some terrible decisions in life. You hurt someone. You killed someone. What if you aren't innocent at all, but you know in your heart that you are guilty?

I want to discuss the life sentence. Most men don't have wise counsel in their lives, mentors - other men they can go to and tell the naked truth, no matter how bad, ugly or disgusting. They can't go and confess because they don't trust anyone with that level of vulnerability. As a result, they are locked in a prison cell of the mind, and heart, and their cell mate is their offense. They are stuck in this cell with their infraction, and every day they are forced to look at the worse part of themselves with no remedy to fix what they did wrong. Because they are locked away in the prison of their offense, they have to put it somewhere, they desire to alleviate the guilt of what they did, but they don't know how to. They are the only ones who know how deep the issue, or desire runs on the inside of them. I'm not saying they are the only ones who know what they did, but that may be the case as well. Their families and friends are unaware that even though the action is done, those men have no idea how to move forward with life.

Ladies, many times, a man can't connect with you because he can't even find himself. This man needs God's help. God can remove the guilt and self-condemnation. The last thing he needs is his woman to remind him of his past. He needs her to give him encouraging words and support that guides him towards his future. A life sentence can be revoked, because the God of heaven has the power to do so. God is ready and willing to forgive, most people aren't. When a man feels there is no chance of getting out, he no longer cares about the effects of his behavior. If a man believes no matter what he does nothing will change, chances are he won't even try. We must love each other better and be a people of second chances. A chance at parole, in order to prove that we have changed. The prison sentence is a lie. It makes a man believe that he must remain in his current state forever. When people commit suicide it's not because there isn't a remedy for their problem, it's because they've convinced themselves they can't obtain that remedy - that solution that will change the course of his or her life forever. That's what makes a life sentence so damaging. It makes a person say, "Why should I change? I'm never going to get out, I will rot in this cell." Many men are rotting in their marriages, relationships, friendships, and careers. Before a man can ever love a woman freely, he himself must be set free. Free from the prison that he walked into - whether through his own behavior or because he chose to believe a lie about himself. Either way, no one can force a man to unlock his cell. A man must see something worth fighting for on the outside. Something he is going home to, that makes him say to himself, "I cannot and will not live another day in this cell."

Ladies, if you see a man that is complacent in life, you are looking at a lifer. Complacent men don't have any urgency to succeed, because success isn't in their deck of cards. Can he change the hand he has been dealt? Absolutely. But most complacency has been enabled by those that claim to love him the most, and a lifer is a person who has been enabled. These men must be cut off so that the only thing they see are the four walls of their own decisions. Leave a man alone to consider his own actions - by himself - and once he looks around and can't find someone to else blame for his current state, he will find that he must take responsibility for the situation he is in. And hopefully at that moment he will recognize that he has sentenced himself and begin to plan his escape.

Chapter 6

Personal Assessment & Small Group Questions

Personal Assessment

1. Do you feel like you are currently in a prison? If so, why?

_____

_____

_____

_____

_____

2. How can your past affect your current and future goals in life? How can you improve these conclusions?

DIARY OF A MAN'S HEART

3. How can you prove that you have changed and that previous destructive behaviors are no longer an issue or cause for concern in your relationship?

DIARY OF A MAN'S HEART

Small Group Questions

1. Name some prisons that people can find themselves in (not literal prisons)?

2. How can people begin to be freed from these prisons?

3. Do you ever just feel like giving up sometimes? Why?

4. Do you feel that everyone deserves second chances?

5. What would have to happen in order for you to deny someone a second chance?

6. What does freedom in a relationship look like to you?

Chapter 7

THE RABBIT AND THE TURTLE

I want to share with you an analogy about the rabbit and the turtle. The rabbit is known to be fast, agile, and very evasive. Their biology allows them to evade predators with their speed. Turtles are not viewed as a very fast species, but yet many don't know that at short distances turtles can actually have impressive bursts of speed when necessary. What turtles lack in consistent speed they compensate for with defensive protection. Their hard half shell protects them from predators the same way the rabbits speed protects it. I believe that as men we fall into one of these two categories. The rabbit or the turtle. I submit to you that men should be a hybrid of both.

I believe history and "nurture" NOT "nature" has taught us an ideology that the rabbit is the only thing a man should be. The rabbit gets to its destination quickly, it's agile and able to maneuver with expert precision. These are the qualities men should have in life while pursuing vision, purpose and destiny. Although those traits may look desirous and they can be helpful, they are not the only useful traits. I believe that there are hidden qualities that the turtle possesses that the rabbit will never truly appreciate. The rabbit will, without a doubt, get there more quickly, but will the rabbit be able to fully appreciate the process (the journey) to success?

I want you to consider the traits of the turtle: it's not the fastest animal, but it possesses traits of stability and clarity that the rabbit would love given the opportunity to see life from a different view. Rabbits are farsighted, which enables them to see predators from a far distance, but the downside is that they have a blind spot right in front of them. Their eyes are pushed further to the sides, which means there could potentially be some amazing experiences in life right in front of them, or some avoidable potential dangers that they may miss based upon how they are viewing life.

Just because the rabbit has the ability to run fast while traveling to its destination, doesn't mean it should. Let's assume that animals have similar traits and experiences as humans. I wonder if while traveling at top speed, the rabbit has had any time to take in the scenery, to take in the ambiance? The process on our journey towards reaching success, is as important as success itself. The turtle would understand it limits, going slow enough where it can enjoy the scenery, appreciating the journey, with its ups and the downs. The turtle wouldn't move so fast where it misses everything but not so slow that it never moves and isn't productive. The turtle won't allow its slow pace to cause it to become stagnant; in times of danger or in times of need it has the ability to speed up and use just enough energy to accomplish its goal. I believe the wisdom found in the turtle and the rabbit is the ability to discern when to use its talents and abilities and to what degree they need those capabilities to succeed.

Considering that analogy, how do men allocate their time, energy, and resources? I believe men must make a decision not to run so fast that they leave everyone behind, and making the mistake of not enjoying the process of success. We must also not move so slowly that nothing gets done or we miss opportunities as they present themselves. I believe that the turtle's physical protection is both positive and negative. The turtle is carrying a shell on his back, he moves slower because the shell is hard and heavy, but it's also the very thing that can be used against predators as a safe haven to regress into in times of trouble. The fast rabbit doesn't have the burden of carrying a shell, but as a result it is exposed with nothing but its speed to protect it in times of danger. The shell around the turtle provides protection that allows it to endure the seasons of life. This shell for a man is the ability to have relationships around him that can help protect him through all of his seasons. Though it may take time, energy, and honesty to maintain them, it's worth the protective benefits these relationships provide. I believe men must have the wisdom of the turtle, and the strength to carry the shell. A man who uses speed, vision, patience and protection as tools in their toolbox are wise men. I want to admonish all the men reading this book to always have the courage to carry their shell for themselves and those they love. To all of the amazing women that are reading this book, be mindful to always encourage the men in your life, whether it's a father, brother, husband, son or friend to always have the boldness to carry their protective shell. They need to engage in and maintain in mature relationships that keep them accountable. Powerful women encourage their men to live life and manage their bursts of speed -

always being on the go but knowing how to enjoy the journey along the way.

Men, we have to do one of the most important things anyone could ever do, and that is define the word "fulfillment" for our individual lives. It is my hope and prayer that fulfillment isn't just materialism, but something that would include a nucleus of people in your life that adds great value psychologically, emotionally, physically, and spiritually.

Chapter 7

Personal Assessment & Small Group Questions

Personal Assessment

1. Are you the rabbit, the turtle, or hybrid of the two? Why?

_____

_____

_____

_____

_____

DIARY OF A MAN'S HEART

2. Do you speed through life? Do you consistently pause to enjoy the moment? Or, do you move slowly and rarely complete what you know you should?

_____

_____

_____

3. How can you pace yourself better than you
   have in the past?

_____

_____

_____

_____

_____

_____

_____

DIARY OF A MAN'S HEART

Small Group Questions

1. Why should we pace ourselves in life?

2. What are the dangers of making quick decisions without knowing all the facts first?

3. Which do you value more: speed, or endurance?

4. How can living like the rabbit help and/or hurt us?

5. How can living like the turtle help and/or hurt us?

6. How would living like the rabbit and the turtle simultaneously promote healthy relationships?

Chapter 8

WATER BREAK

There is a time to start, pause, and stop. I truly
believe that, as men, we cannot drag people through
our lives. Especially - our families. There is an
analogy of a runner who runs marathons (26.2
miles) for a living. It takes the average male runner
4.2 hours to complete a marathon. While running
for this long period of time, each runner loses
liquids rapidly through perspiration. Throughout
every marathon there are water stations which
provide runners with necessary hydration at key

points in the race. The runners don't stop running to drink the water, but cups are available to grab as they pass by. These water stations are kind of like markers to let runners know there's relief somewhere in the near future. I believe that most men do not successfully set up water breaks for their families as they pursue this thing called success.

Most men run like rabbits but do not process and plan like the turtle. I believe "water breaks" will allow our families to have a more healthy and productive life. Without water breaks, families break down and dry up; family members give up and eventually break up. When our bodies are deprived of water they eventually shut down; we become lethargic and dehydrated. If this goes on long enough, our organs will begin to fail. If not replenished, we could experience death. I believe people in every career needs breaks in life. So, why the marathon analogy? Well, I believe many men are so accustomed to pretending that they're willing to go through life running hypothetical marathons without water breaks. All the while pretending that everything is ok just to save face and protect a false narrative, versus saying that areas of their lives are dehydrated, unhealthy and they don't want to pretend any longer. So, many men have become numb to living the lie and they will allow others to believe that everything is perfect. But on the inside they're dying at the core. I believe it requires a special person to look at his life and assess if they are actually on the path to true fulfillment. Truth requires great integrity and character. It requires you to say, "This is where I am; this is what I want to be," and to ask, "Am I willing to do whatever it takes to get there?" So, are you willing to admit what problems truly exist? Are you willing to make the adjustments necessary to accomplish the purpose and plan that's been placed on the inside of you?

Water breaks mean that a man understands where he is in life and he refuses to drag people into the issues he hasn't worked out yet and call it a family. Water breaks allow for a healthy life. Water breaks are like tune ups for a car. Many of the lights that flash on in the car, point to an issue that we can't see with our naked eye all of the time. Those lights tell a bigger story. Ask yourself, "In my life and family, what warning lights have been flashing, and yet I haven't gotten a checkup?" If you keep running, driving, moving without the "water break," or the "tune-up" your life will begin to break down.

Activity does not always equal productivity. Doing a thousand things does not mean you're successful. Many times, people stay super busy because they know if they ever slowed down everything will fall apart. We've fallen in love with busyness versus an actual person, we've fallen in love with a perpetual process that can potentially become unhealthy. Slowing down forces us to address ourselves, our families, our marriages, our friendships, and the quality of our lives. Can we make a decision to be brutally honest? To slow down and to challenge ourselves, to tell ourselves the truth and have the guts to make the hard decisions? So, does that mean we don't run and grind? No! It means we run intelligently, intimately, and honestly.

Living a life in pursuit of some type of goal, vision, or passion is detrimental, but there must be balance in a man's life. Sometimes those goals, visions, and passions, are inherited from people who have gone before us. Sometimes, we see something that has inspired us to want to become something better than what we have become. For some, the light bulb goes off while they are attending school and they see a teacher, principal, counselor, or athlete and inspiration floods their hearts. For others, it may come by seeing someone acting, or arguing a case on television when destiny awakens in their hearts. Whoever or whatever has caused the doors of your destiny to be awakened, we all should be forever grateful. Their talents and gifts inspire us to become greater and greater updated versions of ourselves.

Many men just join the rat race because we were always taught that's what we are supposed to do. I want to pose the question: men, are we working to live or living to work? I believe the answer to that question will truly dictate how we wake up in the morning and the view that we take as it relates to success. Many of us are just living everyday just to work, knowing there's a greater purpose working, knowing that I am at this job, career, or vocation to do something greater. To fulfill a purpose; there are plenty of people that are willing to spend all their time making money, for the primary purpose of buying stuff. - whether it's houses, cars, or trying to keep up with other people. Many times, it's in an effort to please someone that we shouldn't try to please in the first place. Every day we wake up we're leaving to go to a job to pay for materialism that surely never brings us lasting fulfillment. I believe that many of us are so up-and-down, having no contentment, because we are so focused on gaining things versus becoming someone.

Many times our job is connected to our identity as opposed to our identity determining our job. Many of us understand the value of being a good man; we desire to provide for our families, so much so that some of us find a job and stay there forever in fear of failure. We work as hard as we can and we stay there in most cases as long as necessary to have the ability to say, "I'm a good man and I've done my job." And yet we put off hidden dreams and desires. So, we attain a certain level of success and yet we have no fulfillment. Our lives eventually come to a stalemate, and we really stop climbing the mountains in our lives. When a man is no longer willing to challenge himself by facing mountains, he will adapt to the plains of life. He will adjust, but he will secretly always have one eye on the mountain, wishing he could climb, wondering how high he could go if he was able to run unencumbered. As men, we all run at different paces, and yet we all have ingrained in our DNA the desire to be conquerors. We have a genetic code that says we can overcome, that the best is yet to come, that today is not the last day. To a real man, death, loss, closed doors, and missed opportunities don't mean the journey has ended; it just means there's new territory to conquer and new paths to explore.

As men, we must learn how not to allow our job to become our identity. We must allow our identity to dictate what jobs we take, as well as what career paths we choose. This means sometimes having to sacrifice and do what we must do today, so that we can do what we want to do in the future. Sometimes to go forward we must learn how to slow down, count the cost, and strategize. Measuring 100 times and cutting once is always better than measuring once, cutting, and having to repeat the process to correct your mistakes. Many of us have made terrible decisions in life. Everyone has a past and most men struggle trying to overcome their pasts in order to pursue their future. I want to challenge every man reading this book to realize that your identity is not found solely in the collection of your past mistakes but your identity can change when you renew your mind, renovate your thinking and decide that yesterday is gone, today is waiting and the future is yours! Make a decision that my identity will begin to drive my behavior and if I don't like where I am, I can change who I am and I therefore can change my future.

So, passion and dreams are very important. They are equally as important as water breaks. At the end of the day, all men must ask the biggest question, "at what cost?" I understand that we all must provide. If you are married or in a relationship, most often, "time" is a subject of conversation that will come up with your woman. Many ladies have issues with the amount of time that we give them whether it's displayed through physical touch, words of affirmation, quality time, gifts or acts of service. I want to submit to all men that success is a great thing, but before we can consider ourselves successful we have to think about what it's going to cost us and our families to achieve it. There is a cost associated with success and fulfillment. We must ask how much time are we willing to invest and still maintain success and fulfillment. How much money is necessary to maintain success and fulfillment. How will our family function in order to maintain success and fulfillment?

The final, but probably most important concept I want to address in this chapter is our health - spiritual, physical, psychological and emotional. As a family, what's the impact of success going to be on our family's health? There has to be a conversation with those you love. I don't believe that we can continue to just tell our families we're going to pursue success, and the consequences are irrelevant. I believe the paradigm has to shift. Men who are truly successful are those that take the time to invest money, time and energy into their families.

Men, we must understand that when we invest time into the health of our families, when we invest our lives into this core group of people, our nucleus, they become healthy and are able and willing to assist us in pursuing success in every other area of our lives. Many of us have bought into the lie that we have to pursue success at all costs. I believe the greatest success is our families, those that we love. This will require a heart check, a life evaluation. We must ask ourselves, do we have our priorities in order? A healthy life is a balanced life

Is it worth it? Is it really worth it, at the end of the day? I want to ask. Are the houses, cars, clothes, and materialism true success? The imbalance, is it worth our most valuable relationships? Are those things worth it if it means the sacrifice and the detriment of our children and family? Again, I believe we have to switch our view of lifelong success. What if we changed what the meaning of success and fulfillment actually meant? What if the new meaning was leaving a legacy of character and integrity? Patterns of behavior that our posterity can follow? Passing along the house and the car is fine, but leaving a strong work ethic, character and integrity as a model for imitation is much more valuable.

Chapter 8

Personal Assessment & Small Group Questions

Personal Assessment

1. Are you guilty of dragging people through your life? (List their names and what your actions were)

_____

_____

_____

_____

2. How has dragging people through your past
   and or present affected you as a person?
   How has it affected your relationships? (Dig
   deep and talk about your regrets as well)

_____

_____

_____

_____

_____

_____

_____

_____

_____

_____

3. Verses dragging someone through your life, how can you better foster healthy cooperation? *(Be vulnerable and tell the truth! This is your moment!)*

_____

_____

_____

_____

_____

_____

_____

Small Group Questions

1. What is your number one priority right now in life?

2. Should this be your number one priority?

3. How has putting this as number one affected your life?

4. Do you allow yourself and your family/friends breaks in life?

5. What happens when our priorities are misplaced?

6. Define successful? What does it look like to you?

7. Is your view of success healthy? Why?

8. In what ways do you need to modify your priorities? How can you establish more "water breaks" for the people you love who are most important to you?

Chapter 9

YOU ARE NOT
THE PROBLEM

This chapter will probably make a lot of people upset, but by now, you should know I care more about helping people than being popular. This part of the diary is meant to let ladies know that everything that happens in a man's life does not have something to do with YOU. Have you ever been in a relationship and life happens? You lose a job; you get sick or have a bad day? There's an issue with your kids, a problem at work, or you're short on money? Do any of these scenarios sound familiar? Because we are all human and life doesn't care who we are; it comes for us all. When life happens, have you ever had people make it all about them? They may ask questions like, "Why are you treating me this way? Why aren't you talking to me? Are you mad at me?" Even if the person has nothing to do with what is going on, he or she somehow finds a way to make themselves the center of your life's problems and crises. Somehow, you having a bad day at work or being quiet has turned into why are you not talking. Or because you are not your usual self, you're being mean or indifferent. Actually it has nothing to do with that person at all. Life has happened, and problems cause everyone to respond differently. This response is not wrong even if it's not how you would respond or handle it, it's just different, but different doesn't mean wrong.

A man's heart, when life happens to him, desires for his woman to be supportive and show more empathy. Sometimes that means helping him process his feelings but other times it means leaving him alone and giving him time and space to process and strategize alone without your commentary about why he's acting different. Is it wrong for a man to struggle, hurt, or need space without having to give a full monologue about why he needs time to himself, other than the reason that he needs or desires it? I believe the true mark of a woman's maturity is to be able to stop putting herself in situations where he has never put her. If his issue isn't with her, she shouldn't make herself the issue in order to be the center of his attention at all times or to ensure that whatever he's going through in life never interferes with the way she wants him to be - no matter what. Maturity says "I recognize that you are struggling," and asks her man if there is any way she can help? "If not, if you need space or time, I'm happy to give it to you, and when you need me, I'm available to hear you out and be there for whatever you need." That's what men need. They need to know its ok to have an issue and go through true emotions without having to defend when, why and how. He can figure out life at his pace without the pressure of causing more issues by actually being human and having emotions.

I know many women may say, "Well, if I didn't do anything, why does his personality and mood have to change and ruin our time together?" Because it's called being human. When people go through life, it takes its toll on a person. Why would you want him to act like nothing's wrong just to make sure your time is never affected? Is that love? Is that truly caring about him? I don't think so at all. I think that's called being selfish and self-centered. It's the opposite of love. It's caring more about what I want versus what he needs right now. I get it. The door swings both ways, but right now we're talking about how women can love and care for their men better?

Men, have a tough life whether you know it or not. The last thing we need is our queens adding to the weight that we already carry. We don't want to treat you poorly or indifferently, but sometimes we have to regroup, recharge, bring our levels back down to zero, and that's very difficult when our focus has to always be you. Please hear me ladies: Sometimes just letting problems be problems and not making them personal is all we ask. Most problems have nothing to do with you, and that's actually a good thing. You're not the issue at all, so don't make yourself the issue. Allow us, in our time, to process life and begin to work through it. You can help, but not lead. You can help, but not make us feel like we're wrong because our mood changes. You can help but not by telling us we're not acting the same. Those things don't work. Sometimes all we need is you without the words. Your presence in most cases is more than enough. I know many men just never want to communicate at all, but just know that is most likely for different reasons than what I've addressed in this chapter.

Never forget, a man will communicate with those he feels comfortable and safe with. It may take a while but it will happen. I'm referring to your ability to allow a man to process life, without having to explain to you or fight with you about why he isn't on his "A" game. Ask your man what he thinks about this concept and just listen to his response. I truly believe it will help him communicate his true feelings when you ask genuinely, with no other motives.

Chapter 9

Personal Assessment & Small Group Questions

Personal Assessment

1. Do you allow people in your life to have their moments? Allow them to be fragile, broken, hurt? Think of a time when you could have done a better job at this.

_____

_____

_____

_____

_____

2. Do you always pretend that everything is ok? if so, why? When things are not ok, what do you do? How do you cope?

_____

_____

_____

_____

_____

_____

_____

_____

_____

_____

3. Describe how the people in your life currently respond when you have a crisis. Then describe how you would want them to respond.

Small Group Questions

1. Do we believe that it is ok for a person not to be ok? Why do we have a hard time allowing that to happen?

2. Do we take it personally when those around us are not completely themselves? If so, what should our reactions be?

3. Do we rush people to heal, get better or move on? What should we do instead? How do we want people to respond to us when we are dealing with issues in life?

4. How can we show genuine care to the people we love as they navigate through the rough waters of their difficult seasons?

5. What does it say about our character and our relationships if we want the people in our lives to get over their problems and heal quickly?

6. Is there anyone that you've pushed too hard because you didn't understand their season and you made it all about you?

7. What can you do to make that situation better?

Chapter 10

WHY DO I IGNORE PATTERNS?

It never ceases to amaze me how many women say there are no good men left, that all men are jerks, all men cheat, all men are dogs, all men are childish, all men have a hidden agenda, all men want is sex, men don't want to settle down, men don't want to be fathers, men don't want to be exclusive. Breathe. I know that was a lot to get out. I've heard it all. Truthfully, after a while, this kind of talk gets kind of annoying and it really shows the ignorance of the one speaking. Uh oh, did I go too far? Someone has too. Because according to some of you, I'm a part of that group and so are millions of other men that you've never even met.

When "some" women talk about "all" men, you are making an absolute statement that is absolutely false. It's a hasty generalization. Have you met and gotten to know EVERY man on the planet? I didn't think so. So you must stop saying what *all* men are and what *all* men will do. What if it's not all men but just the ones you date and/or ones you sleep with, with or without a commitment? What if there are thousands of great men but they don't want you because you think everyone of them is a dog before you even meet them? Has that ever crossed your mind? I can hear some of you now: "Well, if guys weren't like that then I wouldn't say that about them." Well, if many women, didn't act so desperate and make it so easy for men to get them into bed, maybe guys would be forced to change. How could a guy have five or six different women if the women were not willing to have him? I think it's so funny that every man is a dog for cheating, but he's cheating with someone, right? They can only have multiple people if there are multiple people available to be had.

The issue is inventory. Supply and demand. There's too much inventory. Women want respect, and I believe they deserve ALL the respect in the world, but then I see so many of them dressed half naked in the gym pretending like they don't know every guy in the gym is staring at their butts or breasts, come on. Who are you kidding? Women bending over and doing hip thrust right in front of a guy, and pretending not to look at him, to see if he's looking at her. Dogs only bark for meat, dogs are attracted to dog food. If you are only attracting dogs, then I can't solely blame the dog; I blame the dog and the one who keeps putting out the food that attracts dogs. Or, the one who is always visiting the dog pound, and then complains that she only has dogs to choose from.

My question becomes if you don't like what

you are attracting, when will you stop blaming everyone besides yourself? When will you say, "If I keep attracting these guys that don't want commitment, love, faithfulness, friendship, exclusivity, marriage, family, career and anything else you may want, there might be something wrong with what I'm doing? Whenever you find yourself becoming impatient and wanting something really badly, that's often the worse time to have it. The worse time to go grocery shopping is while you're hungry. You'll just grab products because they look good, but if you weren't hungry half of the items in your basket probably wouldn't have even been appealing. You must learn to stop shopping and being available while you're hungry and stop grabbing items off of the shelf that were never meant for you and that you truly don't even want. At some point, you're shopping just to shop. I hope you see my point. I know there are some jacked up guys out there, but who put a gun to your head and made you date them? Sleep with them? Marry them? Tell them your whole life? Fall in love with them? That's on you; you must guard your own heart because guys like them won't do it for you.

I've met so many women and it's sad -- they've been used and abused and now they're bitter instead of sweet, angry instead of happy, rigid instead of soft. And it's because of some stupid relationships that went sour. I want to give you a bit of free advice about "some guys." There are guys who are jerks and dogs, but if you choose get with them, that's your problem. I don't want to hear about it. These are the guys you meet and they're drunk, grabbing girl's bodies at clubs, waking up hungover. They still keep track of how many women they sleep with and brag about it like a badge of honor. If you can't spot these clowns, then you're on your own. And as much as you complain about them, you probably want that kind of guy because you're desperate and they always seem to be available.

But if you're a WOMAN and you want a real MAN, let me share a page from my diary. Real men don't just go from girl to girl to girl. And there are many reasons why. These men are focused on their life's goals, they are rooted and connected with their families, friends and church. These guys are busy pursuing purpose not talking about dreams that will never come true. These men are not trying to date everybody because they only want someone who's compatible with them. They are patient but deliberate, confident but not cocky, they have character, integrity, and they want a modest queen, not some video vixen that just won last night's twerking contest. They truly want the lady in the streets and the… you know the rest. Bottom line they want commitment and a meaningful relationship. Now, I'm sure by now you're thinking, "well show me this guy." I get it. But let me ask you a question to help you take your focus off me showing you this guy. Would you say you're that type of woman? The type of woman this kind of guy would even want? Wait, don't rush to say yes. He doesn't want the drunk girl under his arm; he doesn't want the neighborhood gossip that's in everyone's business besides her own. He wants modesty, intelligence, character, integrity, chemistry, compatibility, shared dreams, and goals. A woman who adds value beyond her curves, but a woman who can calm the storms in his heart, who can tell the bear in him, that he's safe in her arms. To reassure the man when he finds himself weak she will be strong and defend him and his honor. Do you believe you are this woman? Because that's the kind of man you say you want. But these men aren't clubbing all night, closing down bars, and sadly, many of them aren't in the church either. Now, all men don't want what I just described. There are many that will talk like they do but they have a totally different motive, and you must use discernment, pay attention and seek wise counsel sometimes to notice the difference. Many of these counterfeits have even slipped into the churches and they prey on women under the "title" Christian. It's sad. They pretend like they only want to be friends and they prey on your emotions and make you feel like you have a shot but in their mind, you never did. That's because they're using you. They will tell you they're not looking for a relationship and yet they act like they're in one with you but you will always be a secret. They hide behind the fact that they told you that all they were to you were friends, but your heart knows better than that. Because he's calling you, hanging out with you and inviting you places. PLEASE HEAR ME! That crap doesn't mean anything!!! Always assume a man DOES NOT like you unless he tells you he does directly!!! You cannot make that determination just by reading into it or thinking he has romantic feelings based on how he treats you. If he doesn't tell you that you are EXCLUSIVE & PUBLIC, sweet heart you are what I call a secret! Him saying that you are exclusive gives you the right to make it public. If he says you are, but no one can know about it, or only a certain few, run! Because you are probably one of the players coming in off the bench while his starters are resting for a little bit. If you're not the one and only starter in his game of life, don't put on his jersey and don't get on the field!!! You deserve to be #1 so act like it! Don't ignore the obvious warning signs all around you because you want someone or you want something to work so badly. It's not worth it. Take them around your friends and listen to counsel. Your friends and family (if they are healthy themselves) will be buffers for you. They will keep you on the right track. It's not about getting a guy; it's about attracting and spending your life with the right guy. Patience and time are your best friends. Always remember: healthy people don't hang around unhealthy people. Be the person you want to attract.

Furthermore, you have to learn how to be content in all things. Whether you are single, married, divorced or widowed, you must learn to appreciate the season you are in, while you are in it. Don't waste so much of your current season focusing on the future that you don't live a full life right now! People plan so much for tomorrow that they forget about living their lives today. You don't need anyone to make you enjoy your life -- if you are not happy and content with your life without a man, you will be worse off if you don't grow and mature before you get a man.

Potential is dangerous, patterns are real. So, many people are looking at "some men" and arguing, this is the pattern of all men. I totally disagree. I believe this is the pattern of some, and that women can become infatuated with "potential" and ignore a man's patterns. Many of the women I come across don't really have an issue with "men" they have a misconception about potential. You may see a man that looks good, speaks well, and acts like a gentleman, but has terrible patterns. Our queens will be a lot better off if they pay attention, and interview the patterns of a man, before ever giving him the job of loving her in the most intimate ways in a relationship. Potential is what he can be one day, patterns reflect who he already is.

Chapter 10

Personal Assessment & Small Group Questions

Personal Assessment

1. Are you currently attracting the type of people that you say you want? Do you know what you want? If so, describe it.

_____

_____

_____

_____

2. What are the most attractive things about yourself? Why?

3. Have you noticed any patterns in the type of people you attract? If you are with someone already, do you notice any patterns in how you've changed since you began that relationship? Are you the same guy/girl, doing the same things?

Small Group Questions

1. What type of person do you perpetually attract?

2. Can you see any patterns that exist in yourself that could change in order to switch this reality?

3. Is there anything that you can identify within yourself that needs to change, in order to position you for the type of person you want to attract?

4. Would you date or marry yourself? Be honest. The way you are right now, would you be a great companion or spouse?

5. Do you have to pretend that you are ok, in order to avoid having to relive painful memories?

6. What will need to take place for you to address these painful memories?

7. How have they affected your life and relationships?

Chapter 11

BREAKING FREE FROM ME

When I was a young boy, I was exposed to pornography through television and magazines. I was totally unaware of the battle that would ensue for years to come as a result of that exposure. For many years, I would find myself craving it and desiring it. There were times when the desires would wake me out of a deep sleep calling on me to get a fix before I could sleep peacefully at night. As I got older and built a relationship with God I found a war within my members. My body was screaming for pictures and videos, but my heart was bleeding and screaming for help. I was so ashamed of my secret that I never told anyone about it. I kept it to myself and just figured that over time it would all be over. Needless to say, that was a lie. It was only the beginning.

I was a Christian boy, and later a young man, who truly loved God but had the worse addiction to pornography that I'd ever heard of. It all started with the videos and magazines and then when I was about to wean myself off of those, I remember one of my friends saying that if a man didn't watch porn or if he wasn't having sex then that meant he was gay. I knew there was no way I wanted that idea about me to be out in my neighborhood or anywhere in the universe. I don't have a same sex attraction. I have never liked, desired or wanted another man. Even at that age, I LOVED women, I was just a virgin who decided to save myself for marriage and I didn't want every woman to be able to say they'd had me. I just wanted to honor God in my body and honor my future wife. I figured keeping myself was telling my future wife before I even met her that I'm thinking about you, I'm saving the best of me only and exclusively for you. So, sleeping around wasn't an option for me.

But then I thought, well maybe watching it isn't that bad because I'm not sleeping with anyone. That was my way of justifying what I knew in my heart was condemning me. As time went on, I began to feel the weight of watching pornography. I knew I loved God and that I wanted a relationship with him, but that addiction was so strong in me and too deep seeded. I didn't know who to talk to about it or where go? Who could I tell? If I tell anyone would they judge me? Talk about me? Expose me? These were the battles being written on the pages my heart's diary at the time. I even questioned my love for of God. If I love God, why do I do this? Why do I watch this? Shouldn't I hate this? Then, why do I love it so much and right after I watch it, I hate myself for it?

This was my heart's battle! This was the

diary of my heart as it related to my flesh and lust at the time. I remember telling God I wanted to stop, I wanted to quit, and I needed His help! I remember praying so hard and crying in my closet for so long that my t-shirt would be drenched in tears as I cried out to God for him to help me! And the more I cried and prayed the more I watched and hid. I hated myself, I loathed everything about me. In my eyes I was a hypocrite, a pretender, a fake, a phony. How could I say I love God and have this crazy addiction? I'd scream, GOD HELP ME PLEASE!!! As tears would stream down my face until my eyes would be swollen. But again, who could I turn to? Who could I tell I needed help? I had no idea.

As I got older something began to change. As I pursued God more and cried out for help, God finally (in my estimation) responded! It wasn't what I was looking for but it was exactly what I needed. One day after watching the video, I felt horrible as usual and I spoke to God with a whisper. I said softly, "God, please help me." In my heart, I just knew He responded, "I can't!" Initially, I thought,

"Why not?" But I knew it was because I didn't truly want to stop. It's almost as though he was saying, "you say you want to stop, you say you hate it, but that's all a lie. Kenyon, you can't stop because you love porn too much to divorce it."

After this quick talk with God, I fell to my knees and just cried. Of course, He was right. In my heart, in my diary, I say I want to stop. But I truly love watching it, I don't want to stop, and I only said I wanted to because that's what I was supposed to say. Later, I came across a quote from an incredible theologian named John Piper and he said, "God is most glorified in us, when we are most satisfied in him." This quote changed my life! I realized that God can never be glorified in my life, body, mind, soul, conversations, relationships, until I am 100% satisfied in my relationship with him. WOW!

The light came on for the first time. The reason I was attracted to pornography was because I was not satisfied in God; I had an estranged relationship with my Father, and I needed to say sorry and change and pursue Him. I began to rethink and renovate my mind and heart to fall in love with what my Father loves and hate what my father hates. I GOT IT!!! I realized that being free from me meant to be free to LOVE him intimately. And when I found satisfaction in him and him alone, I would no longer treat God's queens like naked flesh or as a sex symbol. I would honor what he honors and reject what he rejects. Satisfaction in him would bring satisfaction within me.

The reason so many men sleep with so many women and can't be faithful or committed is because they are empty on the inside and they desire and crave what will only satisfy for a moment. That's why they can go from girl to girl to girl. It's because they are governed by a law that says they can have whatever they want and if the women agree it's permission to indulge. I can watch whatever I want because I'm grown. That's not true. These women who allow us to sleep with them are lost themselves, they are lonely, UNSATISFIED in

God and every time we connect with one of God's daughters for pleasure versus commitment, we are telling them and the world, that they are not worthy of a lifetime commitment - that they are only worthy of empty promises and sexual favors.

Women must investigate the darkest corners of their lives; the same way men have to investigate theirs. This will let both sides know what hidden battles and wars are being fought in the shadows of our hearts. We can overcome, but it requires a total surrender of our desire to be *happy*; that idea must be forfeited and replaced with the desire to be Holy. And that comes at a great cost of one's self. But it's worth it. Ladies, if a man is willing to die to himself, he'll be able to live freely with you.

Men don't always show up to you all in one piece. I'll briefly explain. A man's physiology can be present with you but his psychology and emotions can be lagging behind. This doesn't mean he doesn't love you, it means he's only able to give you a portion of himself at that moment. Sometimes a man cannot catch up in time before you show up. His body is present, willing and able, but you feel distance because his emotions haven't caught up to the maturity to match his body. The "moment" is where you are currently, mentally, emotionally and physically. This "moment" is where you desire him to be, but it's not possible right now. So, you either wait, hoping his emotions catch up or leave him and run the risk that he may mature one day and you lost out on the full man you always wanted. Can you see it? Life is full of choices and many times we are choosing between two insufficient ones.

Asking hard questions, will help curb the risk. For example, what value do men place on women when they offer sex instead of commitment? Sex over covenant? The answer is none. Ladies, queens, princesses, we treat you the way you teach us to treat you. If you raise your standard, we will have no option but to align. Please see that you are more valuable than your body parts. You are fearfully and wonderfully made, on the inside and out. You are worthy and valuable enough to wait for. PLEASE make us wait.

Chapter 11

Personal Assessment & Small Group Questions

Personal Assessment

1. What does breaking free in your life look like?

___

___

___

___

___

2. What vices exist inside of yourself that you've never told anyone about?

DIARY OF A MAN'S HEART

3. How have these vices impacted your life and your family?

Small Group Questions

1. What does "breaking free from me," mean to you personally?

2. How does someone begin to break free from the vices of life?

3. Once free, how can we remain free?

4. If our bondage in the present or past has hurt people, what steps can you take to heal those relationships?

5. Are there any vices that are unforgivable in a relationship?

6. Why do people hide their vices and or bondages?

7. Honestly, would a person be safe if you were the only person to know their most intimate secrets?

Chapter 12

HOW GREEN IS YOUR GRASS?

In life, everything around us is either dying or growing. I believe that every area of our lives that receives proper nutrition will not only grow, but thrive. Have you ever heard of the expression, "The grass isn't always greener on the other side?" I think we should be asking, why is that grass greener? Why is the grass healthier? Why does someone else's lawn seem more desirable?

I want to submit to you one misconception. Sometimes people mistake artificial grass for what appears to be real, healthy grass. Artificial turf isn't real grass, furthermore, it isn't affected by the elements of life. It's fake. Artificial turf is made up of material that doesn't naturally grow on its own, nor is it nurtured by the earth itself. As a result, artificial grass always looks healthy, it doesn't go through dry seasons like all real grass. It has all the signs of life and it even looks real. You would never know that it's fake until you get close enough to see it's quality. You don't know the true nature of the grass until you handle it in your hands, feel it, touch it, smell it, spend time with it. When you become intimate with what is artificial, you begin to yearn for something authentic. There are people who look over the fence at someone else's lawn and desire it, while others say they love their lawn without fully understanding what it's soil and root system is made of. You can see pretty grass and not fully understand that there are hidden forces that can be deadly to the life of the entire lawn. This concept doesn't just cover relationships, it's applicable to the individual lives of men all over the world. Anything that grows is being fed - whether it's relationships, or just your own individual life. Whatever you feed grows. Maybe the relationships, and even our own lives fall apart because the proper nutrition isn't being applied. We shouldn't be envious of others, their relationships, marriages or families. We should be asking ourselves what and how are those marriages and families being fed.

Many men are living their lives and leading their families, while simultaneously dying on the inside of starvation. They are dehydrated and malnourished intellectually, physically, spiritually, emotionally and psychologically. So many men are the living dead because they don't feed themselves but live to feed everyone else. Men, have you ever sat back and asked yourself, "Why?" Why am I doing what I'm doing? Is it for fame? Money? Sex? Admiration? Love? At the end of the day, on our death beds, what really matters? These are the questions that we have to ask ourselves as men. We

can make all the money in the world and have sex
with countless women, but what does that really do?
Give a moment of pleasure? Allow us to buy stuff?
What real, true value is found in what we do? That
question to me will tell the truth about how green
our grass really is. Think about it.

There are several basic elements that cause
grass to be luscious and healthy: sun, water, carbon
dioxide and minimal disturbance. With these basic
needs met, there is a solid foundation for a lifetime
of health. When asking, how green is our lawn? We
must first recognize and understand the personal
basic elements necessary to make us healthy. I
submit to you that most men don't have a clue as to
what their basic needs are. As a result, we complain
about not being fulfilled and we continually say that
our needs are not being met. The only problem is
that if someone asks us what those needs are, we
have no idea. Are we ashamed to communicate
those needs truthfully? The lawn has a proven
system that works. If these elements are provided to
the grass, success is highly probable. If this

knowledge is shared, and understood wouldn't your probability of success increase as well? Men, we have been taught wrong. We have been taught that any type of emotion is wrong. We are willing to show the "tough" emotions. Based upon the context, these traits are praised and yet, most men can't handle balancing these emotions. Even though these emotions can be helpful, they can also be harmful. For example, using uncontrolled anger towards your wife or children is very dangerous. But, using anger to fuel healthy change is a great use of this emotion. Most emotion can be positive and negative, based upon the execution. Now imagine the man using the "weaker" emotions. Love, empathy, fear, joy, happiness, sadness. These are powerful emotions, again, if used correctly and in the proper context. As men, we can't be afraid, to share from our hearts, those elements which must be present in order for us to lead a healthy life.

I'm not sure about you but if you've ever spent any amount of time around grass, you'll find that "weeds" always find a way to spring up. Most people don't know this but a weed is a plant, just like the ones you purchased to grow in your garden. What makes a weed a weed is the value placed upon it and where it is planted. In essence, a weed is a valueless plant that shows up where it is not wanted. In most cases, people will do one or a combination of three things once weeds are discovered. They will pull the weeds, or they may use fertilizer to kill them. Some people may just let the weeds remain and run over them with the lawn mower while taking care of their lawn - pretending like the weeds are not there,

I want to talk about the fertilizer. When thinking about the elements needed for us to succeed, we must also talk about the elements that cause us to fail. Because men are typically associated with ego or issues of pride, we are not readily making our issues or struggles known to the world. Just like there are many things required to nurture the man, there are also many vices that can bring him down as well. In other words, there can be a variety of "weeds" that show up in a seemingly healthy "lawn." You have dandelions, crabgrass, poison ivy, prickly lettuce, lamb's-quarters, common ragweed, common purslane, redroot pigweed, and the list can go on and on. This just goes to show that a "greener" lawn has many forces to combat in order to stay healthy, and so does a MAN!

When unwanted weeds enter a person's lawn, people who use fertilizer are aiming to kill at a deeper level than just cutting off the visible portion with a lawn mower. Those who pull the weeds from the root or use fertilizer are going below the surface, and this means getting dirty. They want to make sure these unwanted plants can no longer suck the life and nutrients from green, healthy lawn around it. In life, most men are not taught to pull out the weed, or use fertilizer, they are taught to cut the grass. Just make the problem appear to go away. This is why a man can be quick to fight, but struggle to articulate what's truly causing his anger in the first place. Many men have inadequate tools with which to build their lives, and bring resolution to problems.

When the weeds are removed, it allows the grass to grow to its fullest potential without any restrictions. As men, we must learn how to fertilize our lives, we must learn how to remove things that are toxic to our souls and toxic to our families. Sometimes the things we have to remove are very difficult but necessary. It could be our old relationships, behaviors, conversations, friendships, hangout spots, or mentalities. At the end of the day we should be able to look at our grass and know that we have spent the appropriate amount of time cultivating and watering it. This is success with fulfillment. I like to call this, ultimate success.

And lastly, a healthy lawn requires minimal trampling or disturbance. This means not allowing people to put their negative words, opinions, ideologies or insecurities into your soil. Men should never allow anyone to trample on their grass. Real men are willing to take a stand and decide to support their families and be the men they know they should be. Never allow anybody to judge you, talk down to you, or demean you because you chose to water your grass, to love your wife, to be present for you children, and to live a faith-filled life. Never apologize for being planted where you are planted. Don't allow people to walk on your grass, because when they walk on your grass, they are walking on you.

Chapter 12

Personal Assessment & Small Group Questions

Personal Assessment

1. In what ways in life have you believed that someone else's grass must be greener than yours? (Give examples)

_____

_____

_____

_____

2. How did/does this lack of contentment affect your relationships?

3. Do you know what elements are necessary to produce a mature man/woman? (Explain)

Small Group Questions

1. Is the grass always greener on the other side?

2. How do you know when the grass is real?

3. How do you know when the grass is artificial?

4. Is your grass real or artificial?

5. Is it possible to be both?

6. Is it ok for a man or woman to look at someone else's grass?

7. How can we make our own lawns irresistible?

8. Can real grass at some point just cost too much to maintain?

9. Is there ever a point where the lawn just isn't worth it anymore? Or does that even matter?

Chapter 13

EMPTY SEAT

Many times, when we go to a restaurant, doctor's office, or mall, our legs get tired from so much walking. And when this happens, we look for an empty seat. When we find one, our eyes light up and we immediately think about the relief that a chair will bring. Most of us believe that any empty seat we come across is fair game and we make our way to immediately sit down. We sit down for a moment's rest, making an effort to regain a little energy, maybe even to enjoy a pause in an otherwise hectic day.

But what happens when that empty seat was never designed for you to begin with? What happens when you sit in a chair that has been held or reserved for someone else? Do we believe that every seat is designed for us to sit in? Does every chair have the correct makeup to hold the weight of our lives? I believe many of our struggles arise relationally because we sit down in chairs that were never meant for us. The structure of the chair was never designed for our bodies, the dimensions were decided without us in mind, and the material would make our lives uncomfortable and miserable. Men, many of our issues come because we saw an empty seat in the form a single woman and we believed it was appropriate to sit down.

How often do we find ourselves willing to sit down on any available seat? Sometimes we believe some level of comfort is better than none, even if the chair will never truly support us. What if our design, emotional wiring, psychological makeup, relational DNA, or emotional quotient is designed to have a metal chair? I submit to you; we better find the "right" metal chair. Our problem is that we see a wooden chair and just because it's available, we go sit in the wooden chair. The wooden chair can never be or feel the same as the metal chair. Nor, will it bring true fulfillment, only a moment of satisfaction.

We must never forget, yes, a man wants a great sexual relationship, but he also wants love, acceptance and companionship. Unfortunately, he may not be mature enough to know how to articulate his emotional and psychological needs. Many men are only taught in the context of physicality, how to treat their natural bodies by exercising and staying in shape. And yet many men have the emotional, and social maturity of boys. So, as it relates to the chair that we sit in, it must be custom-made. The correct chair will be able to handle the areas of our lives that are underdeveloped. We must have a chair that fits us at our current capacity, but also allow for space and strength to handle the man we will become in the future. The metal chair has certain specifications, and is made from specific material to ensure it can support the weight of the man. All chairs are not the same. Men are similar but no one is exactly alike. That's why it's so important to know what the "man" is made of before you purchase. If you are looking for that metal chair that has been proven over time, you must investigate to ensure that your purchase matches your expectation.

Now, women, let me help you a little bit. So many times, I hear women say how they've been hurt by men and how they've been damaged by men and how many men have done them wrong. Allow me to submit something to you. Many times, when you've been walking through life, you crossed paths with an empty chair, and what did you do? Sometimes the same thing men typically do. You sat down. You just sat down because the chair seemed strong, nice, attractive, educated, stable, sweet, respectful, attentive, affirming, complimentary. Only you know why you stopped and took a seat. No matter why you stopped, YOU stopped. You can't blame everything on the man.

The fact that you stopped, makes you a part of the equation as well.

If you're honest, you saw that chair and initially didn't even question whether the chair could support your weight or not. Many times, you sat down never checking the stability of the chair. You never made sure the bolts were screwed in all the way, and you sat down sometimes because someone noticed you and made you feel wanted, not knowing the moment of relief would turn into a lifetime of tragedy. This same scenario goes both ways - for men and for women. Most of the chairs in our lives break - not because we sit down in them - but many were broken or weak before we even showed up. The chair hadn't been tested for reliability and strength before we sat down, so it broke because it had defects. Things that have defects must be sent back to the manufacturer, to the creator, back to the source of its design. Many times, men and women believe, they can just fix the chair. I can just strengthen the leg, I can just repaint it, I can just sand it down. I can go ahead and just put some more metal on there or some more wood to make it more sturdy. We can't give fake and phony appraisals and wonder why the product doesn't stand the test of application. Many women are giving their bodies, time, emotions, strength, power, intelligence, glory, which are very valuable, to something that's defective. Women, you cannot continue to spend top dollar for a defective item. You must be honest enough to read the REAL blueprint (who they really are), and decide if this is the life or relationship that you want. Sometimes, a person may need new packaging, or a small repair. Other times you just need a new product.

We must learn to accept the fact that every "package" or "person" that shows up isn't designed for us to open. So many people are opening packages that they know they never ordered. But, because we are nosey, we just want to peek at what's in the box. As a result, we open the box and make something that should've been temporary, permanent. It should have been in my possession only long enough to send it back. You look up and five years later you're still complaining about the package that you opened, but never ordered. I hate to say this but so many men will allow you to unwrap them, or allow you to sit down onto the chair of their lives knowing that you will fall, because they can't hold the weight of your life. But, for the satisfaction and joy of watching you sit and entrust your most intimate self to them, they will invite you to sit down. He loves the way that your body feels when you rest upon his chair, knowing that the weight, not of your body, but of your life is now in his control. We focus on the sensitivity and the physicality of your body, while ignoring the fact that when it's over we're not dropping a body, we're dropping a person. There are millions of men who don't mind being with you, even though they know you will be damaged as a result. These are what I call underdeveloped and immature men. These men don't have the emotional maturity, spiritual maturity, or psychological maturity to love you right. A man's relationship with God, will be reflected in every area of his relationship with you.

If a man doesn't have the humility to look up, he will have no problem in pulling you down.

A mature man knows himself. He acknowledges his limitations, weaknesses, struggles and sins, he knows where he needs to grow up, and is aggressively pursuing a strong Godly character and integrity. A mature man will warn you before you sit in his chair, even though his seat is empty, he knows intimately that it's not ready to be occupied. A real man knows the nature and the state of his seat. He will never allow a woman that he is not able to support, carry, cover, love, or hold up to sit in his empty chair. His chair is his life, and just because it can appear empty, isn't a license for just anyone to come try to occupy it. Consider another analogy that is similar to that of an empty chair - an empty house. When you walk into a house that doesn't belong to you, you are one of three things: a visitor, burglar, or squatter. Both, are illegal.

So, to conclude our original thought. There are good men and there are good women. Many times the problem isn't even a faulty seat. Many times, a man or woman will allow the wrong person to sit in their seat and get comfortable. Then out of nowhere, Mr. or Miss. right walks by and they never even pay attention to your chair because your chair is occupied by an imposter. To the passer by, it looks like someone already owns that seat. Sometimes we miss out on a great thing because we were willing to settle for anything that would fill a void. Many of our complaints about good guys and good women are nothing more than a reflection of our inability to be patient.

As a woman, at some point, you must ask yourself, "Why am I complaining about the fact that every man I meet is no good?" If you find yourself repeating the same scenarios, just with different men, what's the true common denominator? Women are so quick to blame men for the brokenness that's found in many relationships, but I have to insert the notion that if you had similar experiences with five men, and none of them worked out, does that say anything about you as well? I'm not saying they were right, or perfect, but what does it say about the woman who allowed those men into her life? Maybe, those men were able to see something in you, that you refuse to see in yourself. Maybe, the hidden thing in you, manifests itself in ways that you are not ready to acknowledge or change.

I say this because good men are willing to sacrifice with their women to make things work. They believe the ideology that if they make the bed, they will sleep in it. They know who they allowed to sit in their chair, they just assumed that the person sitting in their chair would continue to grow as a person and mature as they grew together over time. But sometimes that man will look at that chair and realize that there has been zero growth over a course of years, and they deduce in their minds that the person sitting in the chair has gotten comfortable and takes the stability of the chair for granted. Some men, will see, feel, and hate this scenario. As a result, many men will pull the seat right out from underneath their women and allow you to fall on your butt, in order to prove to you that they were doing something to hold you up the whole time. When a person doesn't understand the value of something, it's inevitable for them to abuse it. There is a great quote that I once read by a lady named Sarah May Bates. "When you're not acting in alignment with WHO YOU TRULY ARE, you are **abusing** yourself."

Chapter 13

Personal Assessment & Small Group Questions

Personal Assessment

1. List and explain some of the "chairs" you've sat in over the years. What were the outcomes of those relationships?

_____

_____

_____

_____

2. What rules/parameters do I have in place that govern whether or not I will sit in a chair? (If you don't have any, now is a good time to create them.)

_____

_____

_____

_____

_____

_____

_____

_____

_____

3. Explain in detail what a healthy chair looks like to you? Do you measure up to this description? How so or why not.

DIARY OF A MAN'S HEART

Small Group Questions

1. Have you ever sat in a chair knowing it wasn't for you?

2. What causes people to sit in chairs that they know are not for them?

3. Do you think most chairs are fixable?

4. Have you ever been the faulty chair? Explain.

5. What are the most important materials necessary to create a sturdy, comfortable and valuable chair?

6. What are some of the warning signs that a chair may not be right for you?

7. How can we prepare better to ensure we don't get so tired in life that we sit in places we know are not healthy for us?

Chapter 14

FRIEND ZONE

There's a misconception that there are no good men out there. That all the good seats are taken. I want to challenge that thought, and submit my own theory. I believe that there are many GREAT men out there, but women are looking for them in the wrong places. I believe that if men and women would search their "Friend Zones" they would find plenty of GREAT men and women, that we've decided will never have a shot. Why? "Because she's like my sister, he's like my brother."

News flash: if they are not your biological sibling or a sibling through marriage, you're not related. That person is an option you have been overlooking.

We must ask ourselves, who knows the most about us? Who knows our weird ways? Who do we laugh and joke with? Who accepts us the way we are? Who are we most comfortable with in any situation? Who has stood by us and defended us through everything? Many times, it's your friends. The people who are stuck behind the invisible barrier of friendship. And yet those are the people, you can be most vulnerable with. I'm not saying everyone's mate is in the friend zone, but I believe there are millions of spouses, behind the lines of the friend zone wishing they had a shot. The most honest question a person can ask is, why not him or her? Why not the person that I truly trust the most? We eliminate some of the most trustworthy people in our lives by this crazy notion of the "friend zone."

I found my wife in the friend zone. I was in

hers and she was in mine. We did life together as friends for years. I was able to see her in the good times and the bad times. She saw me at my best and my worse. As friends. We supported each other, talked on the phone, went places, shared our dreams, aspirations, goals, and fears. Over time I had to ask myself, would I ever meet anyone like her again? I learned that she had all the qualities that I wanted and those I didn't even know to pray for. She's absolutely AMAZING!!! Is she perfect? No, but neither am I. And guess what? She was in my friend zone. We finally had a conversation about pursuing a relationship and we were both nervous. We loved the friendship, and we didn't want to jeopardize it. But after soul searching and seeking counsel, I had to really challenge myself and ask the hard question: why not? And I wasn't able to come up with an answer that had any substance at its core. So, I communicated my interest and she couldn't resist me! Just kidding. I was honored that she welcomed my approach and pursuit. She's the greatest gift that I've ever received, and she loves me in ways I didn't even know were possible. I'm deeply and passionately in love with her. And it all started off in the "friend zone."

Chapter 14

Personal Assessment & Small Group Questions

Personal Assessment

1. What value could have been overlooked because we categorize our relationships? If you're single, how can leveling the playing field help you? If you're married, how can you build an amazing friendship with your spouse?

2. What are some of the greatest lessons you've learned from your closest friends? Are there any friendships that you wish you could still have? How did you lose them? If possible, how could you go about repairing them?

DIARY OF A MAN'S HEART

3. Do you feel a friendship is the foundation to a successful relationship? Why or why not? *(Think about how a friendship could change a relationship.)*

Small Group Questions

1. What does a real friend look like?

2. Do we trust or closest friends to critique our lives?

3. Do those critiques cause an issue in the friendship afterwards?

4. Why do you think many people put people in "friend-zones?"

5. What happens when you're married and your spouse puts you in the "friend zone" emotionally and or physically?

6. How can a spouse help the other spouse see their behavior and encourage change?

Chapter 15

MARCO POLO
"HE SPEAKS BUT SHE WON'T LISTEN"

This part of the diary is called Marco Polo: You may have audibly heard what I said, but you didn't listen to a word I said? Many men have felt this way at some point in their relationships. I don't know about you but when I was a child we used to play this really fun game. We would get in the pool and one person would be "it." That person would close their eyes and yell, "Marco." The rest of us would all yell, "Polo," and the person who was "it" would have to try to tag us by only using our voices to figure out where we were. Some people are actually in the water splashing having a good time and others are running around on the outside of the pool trying to be as quiet as possible. Everyone is listening to each other to know when to respond because no one wanted to get caught.

When a person speaks, someone has to listen in order to respond intelligently. If a man is sharing his thoughts or feelings, a woman must embrace the idea that hearing and listening aren't mutually exclusive. When a man says, you never listen to me! We know that's not true, it's an exaggeration of the facts. But it still gives an idea of where he is emotionally with his woman or relationship. "She never listens," is a statement that comes with an unspoken tension, frustration and sometimes resentment. In many platonic and or intimate relationships, men have shut down because they truly believed they're not being heard.

In a man's heart, this scenario is equivalent to him talking to a brick wall and expecting a response that will heal his wounds. The only thing a wall can give is the contents of what it's made of. And none of those ingredients possess healing properties. So, many times I hear women say, oh, my man is quiet, he doesn't talk or he shuts down. Or, my man gets mad and he won't share his feelings or his thoughts. Those statements may actually be correct, but they don't answer the real question: WHY? Being able to monitor and recite his behavioral pattern is surface level interpretation, I want to go deeper. Perhaps when he has spoken, communicated and shared his heart in the past, the truth is that you just didn't listen. What if I told you that his silence, isn't a mystery in most cases? What if the unadulterated truth was that his silence is the manifested realization that he's wasting his time, energy, and effort talking to someone that's not interested in listening or understanding him? His past experience in your conversations has taught him that while he is speaking, you're strategizing and planning your rebuttal and or counter attack. So, even before he says one word, about what he believes, he knows doing so has the propensity to turn a perfectly calm evening into World War III.

Remember, you don't have to like or agree with what I'm saying, but if you're really honest, while you've been reading this portion, you're already doing it, and you don't even know me. It's almost natural at this point. I'm trying to encourage you to do a real self-assessment, instead of trying to justify the fact that you disagree with what I'm saying. At least wait until the end of the chapter when you'll have the whole picture. This is what guys are talking about. When a man knows, from past experience, that the content of the conversation is not going to be received, he starts to ask himself, "What is the point?" What is the purpose of continuing to share what he thinks, sharing what's on his mind, his true feelings, or thoughts, when he already knows the response is going to be adversarial? Many times, he will just stop talking because he knows you're hearing him but there's no desire to actually listen with the intent to change.

The healthiest way of communicating is to listen without formulating a rebuttal to what we're hearing - to listen with the intention of gaining understanding. This doesn't necessarily mean you agree, but understanding allows you to respond intelligently. Ladies, this type of response allows your man to know that you did actually listen to what he said, whether you agree or not is a different conversation. Hearing with the goal of understanding and empathy should be a person's goal in the conversation. The verbal response after listening should validate the fact that what was shared was understood.

Sometimes a woman may desire to be right so badly, they're willing to sabotage the conversation in order to prove a point or just be right. As a result of this approach, when the man speaks, he begins to feel that she doesn't have any desire to actually listen. From this moment forward, what happens? He begins to go into his diary and takes mental, and emotional notes. Based upon the subject-matter and the responses, he will determine that certain topics are off limits. He doesn't tell her that in most cases, but a mental note is sketched in his memory of what happened the last time he brought this topic up. He has gone from desiring to discuss his thoughts and feelings, to knowing in his heart that the person he loves the most, has limits to what they can receive from him.

The lady he loves is more interested in being right than having a healthy relationship. Listening is one of the greatest gifts you can give to your friend, family member, boyfriend or spouse. Allowing him to express himself without fearing backlash shouldn't be an anomaly. When a man knows that he's been heard, followed by your promise of working on what bothers him, this will cause for a trust and building block for honesty in the future. A great relationship of any type will always require all parties involved to listen with the intent of understanding, ergo the idea of Marco Polo. One person talks while the other person is actively listening. Listening at the level of maturity that I'm talking about, requires transformation. I view hearing as simply receiving information but doing nothing with it. Listening on the other hand, is receiving information and making a deliberate effort to understand what is being said. Listening will assist in building a stable foundation for one to apply what they heard, in order to grow, mature, and hopefully build more levels of trust and intimacy.

Attacking, criticizing, yelling, demeaning, insulting, teasing and arguing will never bring you closer to a man, it will just put you in the category of someone who values being superior at any cost. When a man's feelings get hurt, he won't express that emotion the same way you do. Chances are, you will never know that you hurt him to begin with. Especially, if it's emotional. When a man's ego is hurt, you know immediately, that's his manhood under fire. He will defend that to his death. But when his feelings are hurt, that is a more sensitive part of his psyche and makes him much more vulnerable. A man who is vulnerable with his woman, is a man that has 100% trust in that woman. Many women don't get that level of trust because their men don't trust them at that level with them emotionally. Believe it or not, it all starts with conversation.

Sometimes, a man won't give you this level of access because you will use the private information as ammunition against him the next time you're angry or upset. This level of vulnerability can be used to make him feel like less than a man. A man doesn't need a prosecutor, judge and jury sleeping with him in his bed. A man needs to come home to a safe haven. The woman has the power to make their house a home or a prison. Many men feel as though their home is somewhere they **MUST** go to every night, instead of the place they LOVE to return to at the end of a tough day.

As a woman, you possess great power to influence the atmosphere of any place you inhabit. Why not become a place that's safe for him? A place where your man can share his thoughts, feel respected, reveal his insecurities, know he is loved, respected and honored. Imagine reaching a place in life where your man can tell you anything. His trust in you is so deep, your love for him is so strong, that he knows the safest place besides God's throne is in your arms. Many times, intimacy with a man is broken because of loaded conversations. A loaded conversation is one where questions are asked and the listener isn't aware that there is a right and wrong answer. The questions are presented in a way where the listener thinks it's totally safe to be honest, and lurking in the shadows is something called consequence, manifested as attitude. If this is indicative of your relationship, then chances are you'll get surface conversations while dealing with your man. When you ask a question, you can't get angry with the response. You can't control a person's answer to your question. I'm a firm believer that if you don't want the truth, don't ask the question.

For example, you may ask your husband or boyfriend if it looks like you're gaining weight. The truth is that you already know what you want him to say. But what if that answer is not the truth? You don't want him to say, Yeah, you know what, you do look like you've gained a little weight." Or, "You know what, I think that dress may be just a little bit tighter than it used to be." BANG! Out of nowhere you're offended. The million-dollar question is why did you ask to begin with? Did you ask him because you wanted him to be honest? Or, are you asking because you really want him to say something that may not be true, but yet it makes you feel good about yourself? This man is doomed to fail unless he gave you the answer you want him to give. If you ask him if you look fat in that dress, it's a yes or no answer. If he says yes, you don't have the right to be mad because you proposed the question. Women must stop asking questions about things if they don't really want the truth. It's almost like training a man to lie. If I ask you certain questions, you better answer in a way that makes me happy. But under different circumstances you better tell me the truth regardless of how it makes me feel. That's just a very confusing relationship, and success is a constantly moving target. That will cause great frustration for a man. Healthy communication requires both people to be able to communicate truthfully and honestly without intentionally hurting one another.

Lastly, a man's answer is exactly what he said. Nothing is more irritating than a woman trying to read into what you said. For example, a man says, "Man, baby, you look amazing today!" If your response is, "What are you saying? Are you trying to say I don't look amazing every day?" What? Where did that come from? To be brutally honest, no, you don't get dolled up every-day. No, your hair wrap that's 88 years old isn't sexy. What are we talking about right now? How does a complement turn into an interrogation? This happens all the time to helpless men all over the world. Why can't a man just say something and that's it? How about a response like, "Thanks baby, I'm glad you like what you see." WOW! What a response. I know this comes off as elementary but it's actually Quantum Physics when it comes to relationships.

Here's another example: You are driving in the car; your man is quiet and looking out of the window. You say, "Babe, what's wrong?" He says," Oh, nothing, just relaxing and looking out the window. "Come on, I know something is wrong, there's no way you're just relaxing looking out of a window." It's almost comical, but it happens all the time. Here's a piece of advice from the diary of a man's heart: Please allow a man's yes to be yes and his no to be no. If he says you look nice, let that be the end of it. Just say thank you. If he says he's just relaxing, try your best to just believe that he has no reason to lie about looking out of a window. That's really all it is. Don't waste your time and risk starting an argument by making something out of nothing.

Chapter 15

Personal Assessment & Small Group Questions

Personal Assessment

1. Explain how you've experienced "Marco Polo" in your most intimate relationships?

_____

_____

_____

_____

_____

DIARY OF A MAN'S HEART

2. Have you found yourself in silence during very important conversations? (Explain) Do you feel that your voice has been silenced? (Explain)

3. In a perfect world describe how you would
   want those in your life to communicate with
   you. What would this dialogue look like?
   What would cause you to feel that you've
   been heard and understood?

_____

_____

_____

_____

_____

_____

_____

_____

_____

DIARY OF A MAN'S HEART

Small Group Questions

1. Can anyone share a funny story that describes Marco Polo in your life?

2. What does healthy communication look like?

3. How do I know that I'm communicating properly in my relationships?

4. What should I do if my conversations have been dominated by my selfishness?

5. How can someone restore healthy communication where there is currently silence or tension?

6. Why is it difficult for so many people to have healthy dialogues about unhealthy behavioral patterns?

7. What do you do if a person sees their behavior is not healthy and they refuse to change? (Married or Single)

Chapter 16

PRISON BREAK

This chapter of the diary will begin to unravel the insecurities of many men. First, we must acknowledge that even though all men are created equal in God's eyes, beyond that, men are different in many ways. Women love to make hasty generalizations of ALL men, when actually, what they see and experience are nothing more than patterns in SOME men. Beyond equality in God's eyes, there are no other absolutes when it comes to men. So, if you approach all men the same way, believing they are all alike, believing that if you've met one you've met them all, then you've done yourself a major disservice and will potentially undermine some amazing relationships.

Let's start with some very practical examples and then we will begin to unpack the more intimate content in a moment. If you go to any public place, you will see men and women everywhere. If you look at the men, on the surface, you will notice many things, even though you've never met any of them before. You'll notice their height, hair, eyes, body type, clothes, weight, wedding ring (or the lack of one), how attractive he is; I'm sure by now you get the point. There are observations that you can make without any interaction. These are the surface features and they are important, but they are not the most important.

Many times, people will put themselves into an invisible prison if those surface qualities aren't the best or absolute most desirable. I HATE to use a number scale, but I will use this scale even though for people and looks - just to prove my point. So, let's use a sliding scale from 0-10. 0 being the worse and 10 being the best. If they see a man that's an 8-10, most women are infatuated and ready to tell their friends about him. Most women can tell who their celebrity crush is without giving it that much thought. And it's almost always based solely on looks. How do we know that? Because most women have never met their celebrity crushes! It's all surface. Many will try to lie and say, no it's because I love their talent! They sing, play a sport, work as an actor, etc. That's just not the truth. I can show you hundreds of great actors, singers, professional athletes that will never make any magazine and their names you wouldn't recognize if anyone told you about them.

People love to say that men are 100% visual. The truth is that we are as visual as women are. My example above gives you a very clear example. The difference between the celebrity crush and the guy who's name you don't know, is that your crush is probably an 8-10 on your surface scale and the other guy is probably under a 5 because he doesn't have the surface qualities/features women find attractive. It sounds bad but it's the truth. Everyone has a "type," or "preference." And there's nothing wrong with that - unless you lie and say you don't. This is important to understand because if you can't tell the truth about that, then you'll miss the lesson that is to come. Now, I'm fully aware that all the concepts in this book go both ways, the door opens and closes. But for this version, I'm trying to help all the queens out there to understand men just a little bit better. We imprison ourselves if we only look at the surface qualities that required no investigation. We place so much importance on how someone looks that we've lost sight of the most important qualities in life - the hidden qualities.

Valuable things aren't just laying out for all to see, touch, and take. Things of value are put away, covered, or locked up. There's a process of identification before access is granted to make sure those that enter are approved and safe. In prison, only the external qualities matter, that's why a man can spend two hours a day in the gym, but zero minutes reading a book that will help him become a better husband, father, or person in general. This is not all men, this is just an insight to how many men think, even if they never say it. Men have the need to be wanted, and if I only hear women comment on the physical attributes of a man, what will I believe is most important to them? I will do my best to be what women find physically attractive because that's they've shown is most important. In most cases, men will hear women talk positively about the external features and because that conversation is in abundance, they will spend their time trying to become what will catch and hold your attention.

What I find the most interesting is that as much as they love how a guy looks, once in a relationship the conversation shifts from looks to how men treat them. Looks were enough to get the relationship started. But when I counsel couples who are in "REAL" relationships, I hear the most complaints about consistency, integrity, character, faithfulness, work ethic, kindness, gentleness, patience, understanding, empathy, and listening. Wait a minute! How is it that the man that physically looks like an 8-10 can get all the praise from women from all over the world, and yet there are no commercials showing his hidden characteristics being promoted as sexy and desirable? I want to submit to you that many women are locked in a prison of commercialized relationships. Movies, and television shows depict actors. A real-life relationship lasts much longer than a movie or television show. Therefore, you can see over time who your significant other is beyond their face and body. They have to work and raise kids, they deal with the complications of life, and real struggles that push and pull on the relationship.

Furthermore, there is no script to follow, no lights, camera man, director, or stage crew, and you have to do all the dirty work yourself to make the story of your life and relationship great. Many women love the "idea" of marriage and never count the cost or the amount of work required to remain happily married. In real life, the main character may be a "5" physically and his hidden character if given a chance would show you that he's actually a "10." I know I might have lost many of you right there. But it's true. Attraction is a very relative term. Please use it loosely. One woman may consider a guy a "3," but the next woman is drooling over him, saying he's a definite "10." Beauty is truly in the eyes of the beholder. A man could be the sexiest man alive, but if he's cheating on you, beating you, cursing you out, talking down to you, treating you like a slave instead of a queen, let's see how long you find him attractive.

This topic is so important because you will find that many men will respond and treat you a certain way based upon the pages of their diaries and the way they believe you perceive the world and men. They listen to you and they formulate an ideology of how you view and want your man to be. You may have never used those words, but that's what he hears. My lady, girlfriend, fiancé, wife, likes "this." The problem is created when they hear what you like, but realize they don't measure up. You can say, "Baby, I only want you." But that doesn't do much when they know that what you have eyes for looks nothing like him. Many times, when you are confused about why your man is quiet, bothered or upset, what you feel isn't necessarily his physical insecurities. It may be his emotional insecurities. Many relationships have fallen apart because of a man's emotional insecurities.

Have you ever been dating a guy and been together with a group of people around? There might be another guy in the group who is a little bit funnier than your guy and he's cracking jokes. In response, you're laughing and just having a good time, but in the corner of your eye you can feel your man giving you the look of death. That's nonverbal emotional insecurity. Even though no words were spoken, his body language told an entire story. What's fascinating is that in this scenario, you could've found him completely unattractive physically, but you may enjoy his personality. This doesn't mean you want him, but to your man, it feels that way. He's asking himself, "What does he have that I don't?"

I hope you can see the big picture. Some personalities are just naturally more engaging, and you're just having a good time, but when your man gives you that look, you already know that going home there's going to be an argument. That's prison break. It's when commercialized relationships meet reality. When you are insecure, it's very difficult to separate people having a good time versus flirting. Insecurity is a lens or filter many men look through. And that filter can cause us to believe something that may not be true.

So, let's unpack an issue that most men are afraid to talk about. Many men lie and deny the fact that they have hidden insecurities. We say we don't have any insecurities because we don't want our manhood to be questioned or appear soft in some way. I can tell you without a shadow of a doubt that every man wants to feel wanted by his woman;

every man wants to feel that his woman finds him attractive, that they're the best man in the world, the reality of this conversation is that there will always be someone who is smarter, more attractive, in better shape, and as men we innately know this to be true. But who wants to verbalize that? We definitely don't want to hear our woman validating this truth by commenting about other men. This is why valuing seen and unseen qualities matter so much. When you see that your man is showing signs of insecurity, hopefully they don't stem from your past behaviors that provoke such a response, but even then, healing is still possible. When you see the signs, don't immediately say, "Here he goes again." This is actually an opportunity to build a healthier relationship. Privately ask him what he's feeling and what's on his mind. Assure him that you won't judge him or tease him. Ask him to help you understand how you can love him better in situations like this - how you can reassure him of your love, attraction and commitment to him and to the relationship.

This type of response to a behavior rooted in unhealthy insecurity, can open up levels of trust that never existed before. This response could be the beginning of a new foundation for him to explore, a new normal emotionally. Prison break as a woman is taking your power back. You can't control his insecurities but you can control how you respond to them. Your response can be the difference between deepening the already existing insecurities or the uprooting of these vile and harmful feelings. Being able to uplift your man physically and emotionally is vital to a healthy relationship. Finding ways to encourage him is important. A man who knows he is loved fully and completely, is typically a man who isn't dealing with unchecked insecurities. His woman's love is so obvious, that he never questions her satisfaction with him.

I believe the responsibility of fostering a healthy, trusting and safe relationship falls on the shoulders of both the man and the woman. I believe that men have a responsibility to protect their eyes and conversations. We must perfect the art of fleeing and or avoiding any environment that can potentially cause our significant other to deem our behavior inappropriate. I believe there has to be an open conversation and a deliberate action plan to reassure her that there is no need for concern. And this is implemented by consistent behavior patterns. If a man is insecure, it's going to take time for him to be able to address the insecurities within himself and to regain his confidence as a man. There's nothing worse than an insecure man, because he will always interpret your behavior through his lens of insecurity even if you've done nothing wrong. Deliberate behavioral patterns are crucial. I truly believe that a person cheats in his or her mind and heart before he or she cheats physically. Our physical actions reflect the symptoms of our souls.

This last part is to challenge the man and the woman. If you are the man and you are insecure, before you attack the woman, look at yourself. Then ask, is this something that I made up, or do I view this situation for what it really is? Am I reading into something that isn't there? And for the woman, before you defend your behavior, ask yourself if there is any level of truth to it? The best way to break out of the prisons of insecurities is by making deposits into your freedom. Make healthy deposits into each other. Daily affirm each other, privately and publicly. Let your social media pages leave no one wondering who you love and why. Take advantage of every opportunity to share with your man or woman why they are a "10" in your eyes. Dig deep, be vulnerable and let them know you need them, appreciate them, honor them, love them, and find them incredibly irresistible! These deposits will pay huge dividends on the day you need to make a withdrawal. Stay free my friends.

Chapter 16

Personal Assessment & Small Group Questions

Personal Assessment

1. Explain how you have experienced prison break in your life?

_____

_____

_____

_____

_____

2. Have you placed value on surface attributes
   and lived to regret it? (Explain) Why did
   you do it? What was important at the time?

_____

_____

_____

_____

_____

_____

_____

_____

_____

_____

_____

_____

_____

3. Have you ever given a rating and learned later that you missed the big picture? Your four or five was actually a nine or ten? (Explain) If you could do it again, what would you change?

_____

_____

_____

_____

_____

DIARY OF A MAN'S HEART

Small Group Questions

1. Can you give an example of a prison that you are currently in?

2. How did you get into this prison? How long have you been in it? Have you determined a release date yet?

3. How can we break out of the prisons of our faulty ideologies and fractured thinking patterns?

4. Do we put too much value on physical appearance? How important is physical appearance to you?

5. If the hidden attributes are SO important, why don't we see this story plastered everywhere?

6. What does a **_ONE_** look like? What does a **_TEN_** look like?

7. What rating would you give yourself? Why? Take this opportunity to dig deep. Consider both the seen and unseen attributes?

Chapter 17

FOR MATURE AUDIENCES, ONLY!

During the personal reflections section at the end of this chapter, if there is anyone younger than 18 in the room with you, please have them exit the room; this dialogue will not be appropriate for them.

I want to start by explaining that there are some people who are raised to believe that it's culturally okay if a man cheats, or has several women. It's not taboo at all, it's actually expected. Growing up, you would hear conversations about "notches on someone's belt," which represents how many women a guy had sex with so far. Growing up, guys might have conversations that include questions like, "Have you hit that yet?" Our culture, for years, has praised and glorified the male's ability to sleep with as many women as possible. What is puzzling to me is that when roles are reversed and the female does the exact same thing she's not viewed with the same level of praise and celebration. She's called all kinds of names. She's not viewed as a conquering queen, but something far worse. Our society has made living by a double standard normal.

This has been possible because we have convinced ourselves that men have a right to pleasure without consequence. Men have the right to pleasure no matter the cost. Men have a right to pleasure at the expense of any woman that dares to accept his summons. It is the lie that men cannot be with just one woman, and that they are born to sleep with as many women as their flesh desires. Self-control has gone down the drain along with modesty, sacredness and holiness. Men violate with their eyes, and lust within their hearts for what doesn't belong to them. By saying men have rights and privileges in these gross indulgences and that women don't are only excuses to continue in these behaviors without consequence. Can you see the problem with this picture? Double standards are rooted in the fact that one person is superior to the other and this mentality will pour into every aspect of one's life and flourish if unchecked. So why do many men feel they can do whatever they want? Have as many women as they want? Never exercise self-control? Test and try as many women as humanly possible? The answer to these questions is simple: Because they are allowed to!

I want to liken relationships for a moment to fast food versus fine dining in the context of sex. When a person goes to a fast food drive thru, the process of ordering, paying and receiving your food is typically quick. You pull up to a board that contains all the items that you can have for purchase; many times, they have numbers that represent combinations that you can have, allowing you to order even faster without having to look at every item on the menu. This board contains photos to lure you into ordering something that wasn't even on your mind when you arrived. After ordering, you drive around to a window and pay for your food. After paying, you pull around to a second window in most cases and receive your food. Once you receive your food and pull off to continue on your journey for the day, most people take their bag of food and open it up to begin eating their food, yes, even while they drive. And before you know it, the food that was ordered not even fifteen minutes ago, is now completely gone.

Now, let's take another example of dining, but in a different environment. We gave a general overview of the "fast food" experience, now I want to discuss fine dining. When you attend an expensive restaurant you typically will have to call ahead in order to secure a reservation. The first thing you will notice is that the price and the ambiance is totally different. Also, the amount of time you plan to spend at this restaurant will increase considerably compared to the fast food establishment. Lastly, you'll notice that the crowd is different. Meaning, only those who are able and willing to pay top dollar for a meal will be there. Fine dining will put a nice dent in your wallet, and you come to this restaurant expecting to pay a hefty price. For fast food, you may pay $7-$12 per meal but at a fine dining restaurant you can easily pay $50-$80 per meal.

While dining at this establishment, you are expected to dress and act a certain way. You normally wouldn't wear shorts or sneakers. It's normally a business casual dress code, at the least.

Upon arriving you would check in, wait in the waiting area, and once your name is called, you would go to the host stand to be escorted to your table. The table is normally dressed with flowers, wine, white immaculate linens, sophisticated dinnerware, and crystal clear wine glasses. The ambience is very nice, the music is soft in the background, and the lighting is typically dimmed to set the atmosphere. You just know that time and attention was given to ensure every guest has a certain type of experience. When it's time to order, most items are à la carte. Once you know what you would like to enjoy for the evening, you order knowing that your food will take around 20-30 minutes to arrive. This isn't because the staff is lazy or unable to execute their responsibilities. This time is required because every item is cooked to order. You will never be served frozen food, everything you order will be guaranteed fresh, and will be grilled, baked, poached, fried, or seared to perfection and to your specific liking. In addition to all that, you'll never have to ask for a refill of a particular beverage because their wait-staff is trained to anticipate your needs.

This experience sometimes can last two hours or more. Many times, it's because you just get lost in the food and conversation. After eating, your bill, typically $150 or more for a couple to enjoy this meal, is brought to your table. Days later you are still telling your friends about the restaurant and how amazing the experience and food was. Even though it was much more expensive than your average meal, you tell them it was worth every penny.

I want to compare these two examples of restaurants to relationships. This analogy isn't to demean women at all, it's an attempt to show the willingness men should have to wait, sacrifice and place value on a woman. This is what EVERY woman deserves! And every man SHOULD give. Many women who are designed to be queens, belittle themselves and sell themselves super short. This would fall under the category of being a fast food restaurant. If a woman allows a man to drive up to her life, and freely look at and assess her menu, she has to be prepared for whatever he chooses to order - which includes the dollar menu. You can't blame a man for ordering from the dollar menu, when you made those items available for purchase. The dollar menu includes, being "friends with benefits," having sex without a lifetime commitment and being in a "relationship" without monogamy.

So, he looks at the menu, "you" and says, I'd like to sleep with you. In return, I will give you phone calls, text messages, gifts, compliments, and dates. In return you give me the most sacred parts of your body. She says ok. In essence he's asking how much will it "cost" me? This is the huge question that is implied, though it's never spoken. This is the fast food woman. The problem is that no man will ever honor a fast food experience; she's just a talking point, about how he stopped by this fast food joint and enjoyed some cheap, quick food. It's not something to invest in. She was nice to visit, but never good enough to call home about. He left knowing that many men stood in the exact same line he just left.

Our queens must learn how to force men to expect a different experience - one where they know before they show up what the expectation is. That the standard is so much higher than what they are accustomed to. This is the fine dining woman. She's priceless, she demands a different type of treatment. She's not for everyone. Men don't approach her frivolously because they know her standards are very high and the cost, time, sacrifice, and commitment are far above average. The fine dining woman forces men to wait, he can't have whatever he wants, when he wants it. He knows, that he must count the cost before he orders. Even when his order is complete, he's fully aware that he must now wait until that meal is prepared perfectly to the specifications that will help him become the best version of himself.

The fine dining woman causes a man to leave her presence without sexual stories to share, but intellectual conversations that challenge him to commit to becoming a better man. A REAL man will anticipate the next date with her because there is still so much to look forward to; she hasn't given him everything. He knows that it's expensive, but he doesn't care because she makes him better. He tells all of his close friends about the overall experience that this woman has made him appreciate. He tells his friends about her substance. She exhibits a strong character, high intelligence, she is articulate, educated, full of vision, purpose, and destiny.

Mature people understand that a person's value is not between his or her legs. One's true value is found in the attributes that are unseen and yet affect your entire life. Men will line up to sleep with a woman, but they also line up to go to the bathroom at airports too. And I can tell you from a depth of experience in these restrooms, men pee on any and everything. The line of men may not be because they see value, it may be because they know they can figuratively relieve themselves on her. Typically the fast food woman is not the woman men want to marry; she just satisfies hunger temporarily, and is usually not healthy for a relationship.   The woman that the real man truly wants isn't the fast food woman that any and every man can get and line, taste, and throw away. He wants the fine dining woman. A real man wants a woman that is uniquely his.

Now let's dig deeper for a moment. Men and women all over the world will find themselves dating or marrying a fast food person, who has grown and matured in life. But just because we grow, move on and get married, doesn't mean that sexual baggage doesn't come with us. Some men are very insecure if his woman used to be a fast food woman, meaning she had had many sexual partners in the past. I've only met a few men who were honest enough to say they felt certain levels of insecurity because they knew their woman or wife had all these sexual partners before them.   This man privately thinks to himself about what you used to do with those guys, and how many men there were? He may never tell you the truth but he definitely thought about it.

I personally know men and women who have had well over 30 sexual partners, and those are the low numbers that I know about. I know someone who lost count after 300. I think most of us can understand why the person who dates this individual may have feelings of insecurity. Most of us are not pleased with our past, and with our past comes potential issues and problems that affect the relationships in our future. Many men have sat in front of me during counseling and said, "I wonder if those guys were better than me in bed? Can I even measure up, figuratively, and literally?" These are the conversations that these men never talked to their wives about, and yet, they were on his mind. This was even after 15 years of marriage and 4 children. A man in this situation wonders if while he was making love to his wife, her mind was on a previous man she'd had sexual relations with. He has questions about the sexual activities they took part in while having sex; did she do the same things with her previous lovers that she did with him? Granted, all men are not the same. All men don't feel this way. Some don't care because it's a social norm while others may not care primarily because their past is so full of memories, that having an issue with her and her past would only spell hypocrisy.

So, what does all of this mean? What if we changed how we dealt with the opposite sex? What if we didn't treat our bodies and sex as a revolving door to something that holds no value? There are many people today, when they get married, will have to face the reality that their new partner has had several sexual partners before ever meeting their them. As a result, some may feel that what they will receive in a mate won't be as sacred or special. Meaning, the man can say no one has had this "experience" with my wife. Most men will never be able to say they've even had one unique sexual experience with their spouse. How sad is that? Is this what we want our story to be? Why would women want to potentially put their future husbands in the position to have to deal with these harmful emotions? A man is going to ask himself if there's something emotionally, psychologically, physically, or sexually that hasn't been given to other men - anything unique that makes him special. Whether men want to admit it or not, they want to feel special.

A man has to feel as though he can please his woman in every area. This is why men will ask questions about your past. They are trying to figure out if they can measure up. They're trying to see if they can handle the truth, the truth of your past. Many men are afraid to ask because they don't want to know the truth. If their kiss, caress, body, sex, wasn't your best experience, where do they go from there? How do they recover knowing that you've had experiences that he can never give you? These are thoughts that many men struggle with, and yet they never share. You can feel the insecurity but you just can't see the root cause. Some men can hear a conversation, see a movie, or even hear you compliment someone, and that can be a trigger to their insecurity. Even though there was nothing meant by it, men's feelings can't decipher the difference.

Some women will tell a man who express those feelings to grow up, get over it, and what they will find is that they are actually pushing him further away. Women have to be able to see the man and know that there is still a boy somewhere inside that full grown adult male. I'm not saying you must raise a "kid." I'm saying, we must all understand that no one is fully developed and mature in every area of life. Sex for a man is important and you as the woman can reassure him and create an environment that reassures him that he is the only one. That you are totally, completely, and desperately head over heels for him and him alone. This is so important to a man. Is there ego involved? Maybe. But who cares if it strengthens the relationship.

The diary of the man's heart is his desire for change. We can't change the past, we can't change what used to be, but we can change how we go forward into our future. A woman has the propensity to create an environment that will give unique experiences to her man that she loves so much. That man needs to hear you say, that was my past and you are my present and future. That you have me wholly, completely, and solely. He needs reassurances that he is important and holds a special place in your life. Queens, don't get angry that he's insecure, remind him that it's a new day, and you have every intention to make that day the best day of his life. When making love to your husband, make love to him like you are taking him to the heavens for a holiday. If you were that woman who gave herself as the fast food example. FORGIVE yourself and move on. Know that you can begin a new normal, that you still have value and are worthy of all the love and care in the world. Both sexes have done all types of things. But we all have to raise the standard. Force men to commit their lives to you before you surrender your body to them. If he truly loves you, he'll wait. You are a mature audience, you know that you can raise the bar, make men grow up, force them to make a real commitment before any extracurricular activities. Marriage is a sign of respect and love towards you. Don't settle for anything less, if sexual activity is being asked of you. The choice is yours. If you are married, YOU can rekindle that flame; it may be difficult but it is a choice. Never stop dating, and creating environments of passion and intimacy.

As you complete this book just know that this is the first step. It won't be easy, but it will be worth it. His diary is worth reading, he has great potential. And you have the ability to help actualize this potential into real patterns by raising the standard, pushing the bar higher, and never settling for anything less than you deserve. Men, it's time for us to step up. To take our rightful place by leading with integrity, character, and love. Let's learn to trust those closest to us with our diaries. It will require everything you have left, but you have what it takes.

Chapter 17

Personal Assessment & Small group questions

Personal Assessment

1. In your lives, which scenario describes you: the fast food or fine dining?

_____

_____

_____

_____

_____

DIARY OF A MAN'S HEART

2. How did you learn about sex? Were you taught that it was something special? Something that should be protected? Or something that should be available to whomever you choose?

_____

_____

_____

_____

_____

3.   Do you have any insecurities about sex? Do you have questions that you are afraid to ask your partner? Is there something you are embarrassed or ashamed of? *(Dig deep, this can be a very meaningful and healthy exercise.)*

_____

_____

_____

Small Group Questions

1. In your circles, is conversations about sex taboo?

2. Should sex be treated as sacred, special, or valuable?

3. The average number of sexual partners in their lifetime is 7. Do you think this is too many or a good median?

4. How would you respond if your significant other told you they're insecure about your sexual past?

5. Would you classify yourself as fast food or fine dining? (Why)

6. What does fast food look like to you? Would you marry a fast food person?

7. What does fine dining look like to you?

Special Thanks

Editor
Ashley Rodriguez
writingrodriguez@gmail.com

Book cover design
Brooke Finister
knoxcreativesolutions@gmail.com

Cover photo
Andrae Reed
day3photography@gmail.com

Help Us, Help Others!

Proceeds from this book will help support many **AMAZING** life changing programs and nonprofit organizations.

These programs include but are not limited to:

Outreach programs for San Bernardino County, CA

Grace Family Church (California)

Mark Graham Ministries

Made in the USA
San Bernardino, CA
02 January 2018